TIME SLIPS

A Commonsense Approach

TIME SLIPS

A Commonsense Approach

Karl Petry

Visionary Living Publishing/Visionary Living, Inc.
New Milford, Connecticut

TIME SLIPS
A Commonsense Approach

By Karl Petry

Copyright Karl Petry and Visionary Living, Inc., 2024

Front cover design by Karl and Dr. Sueli Petry
Front cover photo: David DeCarvalho
Interior design by Leslie McAllister

ISBN: 978-1-942157-58-8 (pbk)
ISBN: 978-1-942157-59-5 (epub)

Published by Visionary Living Publishing/Visionary Living, Inc.
New Milford, Connecticut
www.visionarylivingpublishing.com

TABLE OF CONTENTS

Introduction

Knowing Karl Petry over the course of several decades—you come to understand that you have most certainly found yourself in the orbit of an individual who qualifies for the well-known title of "Most Interesting Man in the World." Now, that sounds difficult to pull off, and seemingly hubristic to declare, but permit me a few pages to elaborate.

First, how we came to know one another. It wasn't a dark and stormy night (little about Karl falls under cliché). I had just celebrated a birthday and here I was—on a pleasant autumn evening—entering a not-secret secret organization. Karl was one among the congratulatory crowd's many faces. Without knowing anything more than his name, by dint of initiation we became brothers. We are life-long fraternal brothers in the Free & Accepted Masons of New Jersey.

Together, we have regularly visited one another's homes, celebrated holidays, enjoyed family gatherings, traveled to conferences and conventions, attended parties and banquets, performed charitable works, and the like. I have even participated in some of his investigations and projects. We have introduced each other to a slew of engaging people. We've shared our high points and the low ones. Karl and his wife, Sueli, helped me through some tough times. Likewise, I've supported them in their endeavors. We have grown into mutual confidants and supporters.

Since that autumn evening, over a shared journey across many years, we have been the closest of friends. Although I moved a fair distance away, our friendship did not diminish in the slightest; rather, it continues, especially with my recent marriage, as my wife too considers Karl and Sueli close enough to be family in all but name.

After reading his books you may come away with an inkling that there is a great deal of substance to Karl. You'd be correct. He is something of a Renaissance Man fashioned as an Everyman. Karl doesn't stand out in a crowd (nor does he try to). Aside from being slightly taller than the average guy, nothing about his outward appearance calls attention. If you were to just watch him from the other side of the room, you might consider him someone who keenly observes his surroundings quietly and in an unassuming manner. You'd probably feel comfortable approaching Karl, perhaps even be drawn to the man with his pleasant, easy-going demeanor. Interacting with Karl, you'll find him warm, inviting, personable, and humorous. If your conversation continues long enough, you'll be pleased to find he possesses a versatile personality.

Part of his versatility comes from the outside, thrust upon him by his surroundings. Karl grew up in Newark, New Jersey, a deeply urban and diverse environment where street-smarts and sociability were necessary for a kid to get by. Familial Eastern European roots in an American setting provided juxtaposing contrasts to learn from, an understanding between the Old Ways with their traditions and the New World's fluid innovative spirit. Vacation time spent away from the city in the Appalachian countryside introduced young Karl to yet further insights. He wasn't raised with a silver spoon; still, he came through all the wiser and more knowledgeable.

Inwardly, Karl is a practical guy. His ability to pick up skills with quickness and assurance lends toward an appreciation in many hands-on interests. Musical instruments, electrical wiring, mechanical tools and gears, construction and architectural techniques, audio-visual technology, business logistics, among other areas, has helped him accrue a fascinating professional background. Rock band member and manager, corporate vice-president, auto repair shop owner, film director and documentarian, forensic videographer, are but a few.

Karl also finds enthusiasm for the abstract. He takes great interest in film techniques, song writing, fine art methods, architectural aesthetics and interior design planning, writing styles, psychological theories, historical accounts, nuances of the law, marketing campaigns, and more.

Much of all I've listed was self-taught. While not an expert, his range is diverse.

Karl is a man you should know. I'm glad I can help you get acquainted.

Now that you have a distinct impression of his colorful portrait, here is its backdrop: his psychic abilities. I do not call them gifts, for while many consider them to be just that, Karl finds his capacities fall somewhere in-between along the gift-curse spectrum. Some experiences lead to exuberance, others to terror—joy and fear both come his way.

Notice I use the plural, abilities and capacities. Mediumship, clairvoyance, psychometry, remote viewing, retrocognition, out-of-body experience, are distinct from one another while under the paranormal umbrella. His first two books go into some details about these.

This book, however, goes into subject matter that any of us can experience, and so many have. No psychical abilities required. It is through a network of people in the paranormal field that Karl gained entry to a formal understanding on the topic of time slips, after he experienced time slips for himself.

As he has helped an abundance of people in their individual circumstances through a wide range of services—as a professional and as a companion, both practical and more abstract—my good friend, with this book, endeavors to help as much of the public as he can. Time slipping is a phenomenon that exists. You may be confronted with it yourself someday. Over the years, he has interviewed witnesses and traveled across oceans to compile this information for you. You'll find this material useful should you find yourself in such a fascinating, yet fearful, situation as he and many others have found themselves. "Knowledge is power," Francis Bacon quipped.

If Karl isn't a most interesting man, then I don't know who qualifies. If this isn't a most interesting subject, I don't know what is.

Happy reading and good luck!

Your new friend,

Jason Vigorito

FOREWORD

You'll find in this book an absence of theoretical discussions to explain time slips. It seems everyone has a theory of what these phenomena are and what they are not. Some (authors) who are dissatisfied with one theory will incorporate multiple theories in their opinion.

The truth is, we may not understand time slips or why they occur. The one fact is that we don't know what they are or why they happen. But if you were the subject of an actual episode, you wouldn't want to hear crackpot academics putting in their two cents.

Ufology suffers from the same affliction. When individuals witness unexplained lights and silent aircraft in the night sky and capture these occurrences with their cameras, their experiences should be taken seriously. Too often, academics dismiss these accounts and offer their theories without genuinely considering the evidence presented by those who witnessed these events.

This opinionated community of self-ordained experts of everything paranormal, who were nowhere near the event, probably spent a good time diagnosing the evidence presented, only to rip apart those who experienced it. Never fear, regardless of what's submitted to them, they have many opinions of what it wasn't, which they will readily share and will never conclude with them saying, "I don't know."

In this book, I've taken a different road. If I don't know about something, I'll say it. If I can better explain something, I'll try to do so. I have a saying: know your audience. If someone is a well-grounded individual not known for stepping out of reality and has or had a respectable career and reputation, give that person the benefit of the doubt. I'm not saying to be naive or gullible. Be cautious but withhold your comments until you've exhausted every aspect of the investigation. This approach, rooted in open-mindedness, is crucial in our pursuit of understanding the paranormal.

I welcome discussions of what time slips could be and how they may be produced. Having these conversations may open new areas to explore and realistic theories worth investigating.

Lastly, Albert Einstein was a remarkable person whose intellect was astounding, and his many theories were proven during and beyond his time; I hold the highest respect for this man. Albert Einstein is also the person journalists, scientists, and media personalities go to when they want to validate their theories, always quoting something Einstein wrote pre-1955, the year of his death. I mention this because when the subject of time slips arises, every television, radio, web blog, article, or book will resurrect Mr. Einstein to get validation of their theory from him. An Einstein verification is so necessary that if you can tie your theory with something remotely said or written by Einstein, all arguments are over, and you've won. No one in their right mind will challenge Albert Einstein.

Maybe it's time to open ourselves to newer ways of thinking—things that Mr. Einstein had no idea of or even dreamed of, things that the future offers now.

In this book, you won't find any quotes from Albert Einstein, nor the ramblings of media figures who claim insider knowledge on this topic. They've never experienced a time slip, and I doubt they've ever met someone who has. I want you, the reader, to gain a clear and unclouded understanding of this rare phenomenon that only a select few have encountered. This paranormal occurrence, known as a "time slip," is undeniably real. We all may have our own theories about what it could be, but no credible person, scholar, witness, or paranormal enthusiast can be one hundred percent certain.

In writing about such a controversial subject and what I can expect from doing so, I share this with you. Imagine a life where you dare to speak your mind without fear of ridicule or of being misunderstood. Imagine no fear of failure or rejection. Imagine the possibilities of letting go and daring to speak your truth.

TIME SLIP

Over the years, I've been called to investigate the presence of ghosts and other paranormal forces. Most of the time, I approach these cases alone. However, when I need more input, I ask for assistance from a paranormal expert like author Rosemary Ellen Guiley or "the English Psychic," Paula Roberts. Emotionally, I've never gotten to a point where any investigation has become matter of fact because each case is unique in its own sense. Even after all these years, I never feel at ease looking into the face of a ghost; it is unsettling, to say the least.

For me, the scare factor doesn't kick in until later. It's when things calm down, and I realize that my encounter has been with someone who has died and that a spirit from the other side felt it was important to make itself known to me.

Fear is engrained in us all; it helps us survive when faced with a "fight or flight" scenario. I don't want to give the impression that nothing can scare me because that's totally wrong. For instance, I have never been on a roller coaster. I wouldn't enjoy a ride that defies the laws of gravity and plummets to the ground at a ridiculous speed, and the only thing between me and Mother Earth is a strap and a grab bar. There is also a good chance that I'll be the one with white knuckles you'll find sitting next to you on an airplane as we take off and land.

Yet, there is a paranormal experience that scares me above and beyond anything I could comprehend, and that is my experience with a time slip.

One definition claims that a time slip is a paranormal occurrence where it's suddenly possible to see the same spot but from many years ago.

It took me many years before I could even talk about it. The memory of what happened to me that day re-surfaces at various times, especially at night when I'm trying to sleep.

I wrote about my time slip experience in my book, *Somewhere the Dead are Singing*. Here is the complete account of what happened to me.

On my night table next to my bed is my White Sound Design clock radio shaped like a cube. I've been staring at it since I slid under my blanket and into bed at eleven. When the digital display showed 3:21AM I couldn't stay any longer in bed and I decided to get up. My wife, Sue, was in a deep sleep, and my cat, Sabrina, lying in her cat bed, looked up long enough to open one eye before resuming her sleep. I turned the light on in the bathroom and saw my haggard face in the mirror. Sue won't be up before seven, so do I return to bed to wait it out? Maybe turn the television on and watch late night reruns of *The Honeymooners* or one of the endless talk shows slotted at this ungodly hour for insomniacs? I chose *The Honeymooners* and a few sitcoms from the 1950s.

These sleepless nights are common for me. Nighttime brings visions of paranormal things I've experienced. This night was especially bad because it brought back memories of a terrifying event that I had absolutely no control of, which could have been lethal for me.

My experience began with the purchase of a used Cadillac Sedan DeVille. I was working as a legal videographer and photographer at the time. My work took me through the greater New York Metropolitan area. Some of the places I visited were not the best or safest of neighborhoods. My Plymouth Volare, which I'd bought for three hundred dollars, was so rusty that I had to store my camera cases in the back seat because the floor of the trunk was so rusty that you could see much of the road underneath it. The last voyage of the

Volare happened outside Philadelphia in Cherry Hill, New Jersey. The A-frame which held the left front wheel broke loose making the car impossible to drive. There was no use in trying to fix it. I just junked the car where it stopped.

The next day in the local paper, I read about a Cadillac for sale. The seller wrote that it was in good shape and only seven hundred dollars. I called the owner and although it was already late in the day, he said that he'd stop by with the car. I told him that if I liked it, I'd buy the car on the spot.

The Cadillac needed a paint job but was mechanically sound. Most importantly, it had no rust. The enormous trunk was a big plus; it would easily hold all the equipment I hauled from job to job. I bought the car that night. While I drove the man back home, I learned that he was selling the car because he was running for public office in Bergen County, New Jersey. The car was a donation to his campaign, so a speedy sale gave him cash for his campaign. It was a win for us both, because I got a great car at an unbelievable price. Soon after, I took the car to the local Maaco auto body shop, had it painted and ended up with a rather smart looking Cadillac.

These large road yachts have complicated electronic systems. The elegant dashboard conceals miles of multicolored wires. One night as I was returning home from a video shoot, traveling down Route 280, my headlights suddenly turned off. At the time, I was traveling sixty miles-per-hour in traffic. Luckily for me the highway was well-lit, and I managed to make it home without incident.

The next morning, I turned on the headlight switch and the lights came on. I went over, under, and around the entire car trying to find a loose wire or faulty switch, but no matter how much I shook the wires the headlights remained on.

That night coming back from shopping, you guessed it, the lights turned off again.

I had a good friend named Alberto, who owned an auto repair shop in the neighboring town of North Arlington. I stopped by and told him about my finicky headlights. Alberto was not surprised. He was familiar with this problem. Rather than take up time at the shop, he asked me to meet him at his house in Glen Ridge at six.

He lived on Hillside Avenue in a very nice, tree-lined neighborhood. I arrived early and parked in front of his house. My Cadillac's red leather seats were very cozy, so I put the window down and the radio on and watched cars passing on the main street just a block away.

It wasn't long before this comfortable setting took a turn for the worse. The ambient sound outside began to fade; even the car radio seemed to be losing its volume, and in a flash the world went silent. I began hearing the World War I song, "Over There" sung by a choir of men. At first, it was very soft, but as the song repeated again and again it became louder each time. The music in my head was now deafening. Hoping to escape the noise, I exited the car. "I'll walk away from the house and car," I thought, in hopes that the music would stop. I walked to the main street, Belleville Avenue.

Across the intersection of Hillside Avenue and Belleville Avenue is the Bloomfield Cemetery. My walk wasn't helping as the song got louder and louder. I passed through the front gate of the cemetery and, once inside, I turned toward a circle of gravestones, which were the graves of soldiers who had served in World War I. Instantly, the music stopped. It was as if the music purposely led me to the cemetery and to these soldiers' graves. Why was this happening to me? All I wanted to do was get my headlights fixed, and now I was standing in a cemetery overlooking gravestones of World War I veterans.

Looking down on the stones I began to get a strange sensation. The stones suddenly disappeared. The lines of tombstones were now replaced by trees. I turned my head to the front gate. It too was gone, along with the metal fence that separated the cemetery from Belleville Avenue. I saw another fence in its place. A wooden fence, not a picket type but long timbers suspended on "X" supports. Belleville Avenue was still there but its surface was dirt. All this happened in seconds; one image was quickly superimposed with another.

Maybe this experience would fascinate some people, but it scared me. Something was happening that I had no control over. I want to make this clear. It was not a dream state or hallucination. I was physically there at the site with the ground under my feet and the wind and smells you would find in a wooded area.

My vision cleared and the ambient sound that I lost just a few minutes ago returned to normal. I was confused; I didn't know what to do. All that I knew had gone, and in its place was another world and another time.

Things went from bad to worse. Now, I could hear someone talking. I turned to my left to see a gathering of people facing a minister reading from a prayer book. Bravely, I walked toward the gathering and saw that a burial was taking place. I got within a hundred feet of the grave when the minister stopped talking and he and the people turned and looked at me.

I continued to walk behind them to escape the scene and found a large stone to sit on. The minister spoke of the deceased, a soldier of the Revolution, and offered prayers for his soul. At different times a woman or man who was standing in front of the open grave would look at me, probably trying to figure out why this man was there and why was he wearing such strange clothes.

I had my own observations; the women wore long skirts that were covered in mud six inches from the ground. Their dresses were colored but faded as if the fabric were dyed with watercolor. Their faces looked old. I'm sure these women were no older than their mid-twenties, but by today's standards they could have passed for late forties or even early fifties. The men's clothing looked crude, and everyone's clothing was wrinkled.

The horror of the situation was sinking in. What started off as a problem with my Cadillac had now escalated into a life-threatening adventure. What was worse was that I had suddenly disappeared from my wife and family. All efforts to find me would be wasted. In reality I was just a block away from my car but in a different time.

I watched as the burial ended and the people walked away. The minister was the last to leave. He glanced at me at least three times before exiting the grounds. I stood up shaking and nauseated. That scary scenario returned to my mind. The thought of not returning to my time weighed heavily on me. My disappearance would cause major concern to all those who knew me, and the thought that I became trapped in a time slip would never enter their minds.

When a person suddenly vanishes, thoughts of foul play are always brought up. Your wife, family, and friends are suddenly suspects in the eyes of the law and of course, the policy-paying insurance companies. On the other hand, now I was stuck in a period without the skills or knowledge to exist in this time. Mentioning to the people of the time that "I'm from the future!" would bring a one-way ticket to the local asylum for the insane or attract the watchful eye of the law and clergy. These unfortunate scenarios came rushing to my mind in seconds. I had to face the fact that I was alone with no one to talk to. Even my twenty-first century American-speaking dialect would probably get a laugh or questionable look from the locals.

I remained on the large rock in the cemetery for a few minutes. As I contemplated my situation, another sound hit my head, a high-pitched ringing. Before my eyes, I saw the wooden fence change back to its original modern-day form. The trees that were covering the area were now lines of tombstones. In a flash, I returned to present day. Without losing a second, I ran out of the cemetery, up the avenue, down Hillside Avenue and to my Cadillac with the faulty headlights. With keys in the ignition and the engine roaring to life, I headed home.

When I got home, I thought, who could I tell of this experience? Sure, I can tell my wife but who else? I'm the guy who sees ghosts or images of the past. All my friends, acquaintances, and family have come to terms with this, but to tell them of my time slip? Nobody would believe it and, quite frankly, why should they?

Why would something like this happen to me? I have a theory that people like me are super sensitive, that's why we have unusual mental abilities like psychic talent, psychometry, and even mediumship. I'll go so far as to say that super sensitivity may even make a person a target for Extra Terrestrial encounters.

Time has passed from that memorable day at the cemetery, but the flashbacks and horrors of that day will follow me for the rest of my life.

Months later while watching a TV program, the narrator of the program mentioned the term, "time slip," and briefly gave a vague explanation of it. I never heard of such a thing as a time slip. I thought that going back in time was a unique experience. However, after watching this program, I soon changed my opinion. I discovered that time slips were a real phenomenon and have happened to others.

One day, I was speaking to parapsychologist Joanne McMahon over the phone and told her of my time slip incident while an actor friend of mine named Mary sat near me. When I finished, Mary approached and said she overheard my conversation and knew of someone who had the same experience, a woman named Marie. I asked her if I could speak to her.

It turned out that Marie was a dance instructor and manager for a dance troupe that Mary was a part of. The troupe was scheduled to perform in Upper Montclair the following week. Mary arranged to have Marie speak to me after the recital.

It was a Saturday afternoon, and the recital was on the second floor of a nightclub in town. The bar was closed but soft drinks were available to the audience. I'm sure most of the people there were relatives of the dancers. I sat in the front row next to the stage. Mary was a good dancer, and I was sure if the others were as talented as Mary, they'd put on a spectacular show.

I was not disappointed. Not one dancer was ever out of step and all kept smiles on their faces even during the most difficult routines. When it was all over, the crowd stepped up to the stage and congratulated the dancers. I stayed behind as one by one the room emptied until just a handful remained.

Mary introduced me and I invited Marie to sit at my table. Mary walked away to join her mother who was waiting at the door.

Marie had a straight, no-nonsense personality. She knew why I was there and was noticeably bothered by recalling her story to a stranger. I briefly told her of my experience at the cemetery and the fear I still have of it to this day.

She looked directly into my eyes and gave her account of her time slip. Her dancers put on a show at an old theater in Vienna, Austria. The audience was very taken by their performance and wanted to meet the dancers in person. Everyone agreed to meet at the restaurant next to the theater.

Marie told the dancers to go on ahead and she would collect and pack the costumes and join them later. Soon, Marie was alone collecting the costumes and draping them over her arm. She walked to the off-stage door that led to the dressing rooms and where their packing boxes were stored.

Marie opened the door and saw the dressing room filled with men and women dressed in clothing from the 1700s. She saw women with powdered wigs in long dresses with narrow corseted waists. Marie walked into the room and the women stared at her almost in horror. Marie was wearing jeans, and the women stepped aside giving her a wide path. Murmuring erupted with these women mixed with gasps. The storage boxes were no longer there, and the dressing rooms now looked completely different. It was as if she was in another theater. Marie now realized she had been transported back a few hundred years. The women started to follow her as if she was a sideshow freak. She threw the costumes at the wall and ran out a side door exiting the back of the building. Her head felt as if it was in a vice with pain radiating throughout her body.

As quickly as it came, the feeling was gone. Marie was back. She went to the restaurant but didn't have the nerve to tell anyone what just happened to her. It took her over a year to tell anyone about her episode.

I could feel she had the same emotions and fears as I had. After she finished her story, she excused herself and left. It was obvious that her recalling the story was just as painful for her as it was for me.

Years have passed since my time slip and I still suffer from its effects. It's the unanswered questions that haunt me. The most terrifying one is, what would have happened if I had remained in that time and not returned? That is the ongoing nightmare that still wakes me in the middle of the night and jars me at quiet times during the day. It may sound trivial but the knowledge of being sent to a time over two hundred years ago and to interact with the population that died so many years before my birth is unsettling.

In short, it's living with the dead. Since then, I have researched the time slip phenomenon. Some will acknowledge the incident but won't discuss it, and I

David Baldwin, d. April 28, 1810. Bloomfield, NJ Cemetery.
Photo by Karl Petry.

found only a few others who will. What's worrisome is the possibility of a time slip that goes unnoticed and is never discovered. Are there some who went back in time and couldn't return? If so, how many people who are missing have fallen victim to this?

It took years for me to gain the courage to re-enter Bloomfield Cemetery and stand at the grave of the man I saw being buried. I know now that his name was David Baldwin, who died on April 28, 1810. In front of this tombstone was a recently placed marker identifying him as a Revolutionary War soldier. I hear the echo of the preacher's words at the burial, "Soldier of the Revolution."

This two-hundred-plus-year-old stone is well-worn and slowly breaking apart. I hope that someday, someone will restore and preserve it for future generations to see.

Setting Goals

Time slips are a genuine phenomenon and have been reported worldwide for years. In writing about this, I intend to bring a true account of this phenomenon to the public. This will be a fresh look at time slips and not regurgitated stories told repeatedly and embellished every time they're told.

Let me begin by saying that when the subject of time slips is brought up, almost always someone will openly share their opinion, whether asked or not, that the phenomenon is strictly a psychological issue and that the person who experienced it is somehow having a mental breakdown and has imagined the entire episode.

There is never a shortage of these so-called self-professed experts claiming to have vast knowledge about paranormal topics or, should I say, ALL subjects. In short, no matter the question, from space travel to nuclear physics, UFOs to global warming, they and only they have the correct answer. Listen closely and you'll never hear them say, "I don't know."

I'm sure you can sense my resentment for these self-proclaimed know-it-alls. Society is filled with these so-called "experts," which is probably why so many people who experience the time slip phenomenon are reluctant to talk about it with others. Just look at what happens to the folks who report seeing a UFO. The hell they go through being ridiculed by family, friends, and even the media teaches them just to keep their mouths shut. My heart goes out to those military pilots who endure intense mental, technological, and physical training, fly multi-million-dollar aircraft, and are trusted with highly destructive rockets and bombs. Still, if they report a UFO, they are often grounded for being mentally unstable. The same holds true with commercial pilots. The rule for them is simple: see nothing and keep your job.

Don't Mess with Time

Since before we were born, the one idea humans have embraced was the concept of time, sixty seconds to the minute, sixty minutes to the hour, twenty-four hours in a day, and three hundred sixty-five days in the year. This is our unspoken law, which we dare not neglect or challenge. We base our day-to-day existence on the law of time. It tells us what time we begin work, our allotted schedule for lunch, and when we call it a day. By it, we know when the bus is scheduled to pass our corner, when airplanes take off and land, and, of course, when to have dinner. We rely on it to tell our date when we'll pick them up and when the show will begin. Don't forget our doctor and dental appointments, and the list continues. We take it all for granted and don't give it a second thought. If we mess with time, the result will be catastrophic. Our biological clock starts running at birth and ends at death; we don't give time a second thought.

Now let's examine the concept of a time slip.

Problems with Time Slip Participants

A time slip happens to individuals at random. What we know is that a time slip could last a few minutes or a bit longer. Explaining a time slip often confuses the listener; they believe you are describing actual time travel. Thanks to television and films, the idea of time travel seems like fun and an excellent, enjoyable adventure. You can tell they never thought this through.

Back in 1967, there was a television program called *The Time Tunnel*. The two main characters in the show were scientists Dr. Tony Newman and Dr. Douglas Phillips played by James Darren and Robert Colbert. They were part of a government program for time travel. Due to a time machine malfunction, the two men were aimlessly traveling and bouncing their way through time. These men were experts in history. When they landed on the seagoing ship, *Titanic*, they knew the date of its sinking, why it sunk, the captain's name, some of the known passengers, and what ship would finally rescue the survivors. Their effort to warn the captain of the ship's fate was in vain, and in the end, the ship sank. At this part of the story, our time travelers disappeared off the ship and bounced into another time. Nice premise for a television show, but let's bring this scenario to a realistic modern-day situation. Should a person get caught in a time slip and be propelled back to a different time, would they know history like these two characters in the TV show? The answer is a resounding No.

Unfortunately, the average person knows very little of history. Using the show as an example, *The Time Tunnel*'s first episode as a starting point, ask your friends and family what was the date of the Titanic sinking? Who was on board, and what was the captain's name? Very few of us know these answers. Years ago, I asked various family members who lived during the Second World War questions about rationing food and their reactions to some of the events that happened during that period, especially the dropping of the atomic bombs. They were unsure of the dates and had forgotten their reactions to many of the monumental events. These were ordinary people who, at the time, were going to school, joining the military, or working at a defense plant. They were preoccupied with passing their tests, training for the military, or putting food on the table. What was happening on the other side of the world and the details of those events did not concern them as much as their everyday lives.

A high school history teacher once asked if I would be a guest speaker at one of her classes. She knew that I was a history buff and that I would often speak at local schools about unknown and unusual facts about American history. She was thrilled that I agreed to speak to her class. I cautioned her about not being so optimistic about the reaction from the students. From my experiences, it amazed me how little students knew about history. She assured me that these were her best students, and they knew American history. I made a bet with her; I said that at the end of my talk, I would ask the class three questions, and if they got at least one right, I would buy her lunch. She would buy mine if they couldn't answer the questions correctly. I added that her worst student would be identified if I heard them say, "That happened before I was born."

I stood before the class and spoke of World War I and the effect it had on the area, including the sabotaged explosion of an ammunition plant in a nearby town. Most of the class listened, and many enjoyed my talk; how much they remembered is questionable. Then came the time to ask my three questions. The teacher stood in the class doorway smiling, "What year did man first land on the moon?" A few called out, "1957," "1965," "1950." I glanced back at the teacher and said, "It was 1969. Next, name one year of World War II." Once again, the dates were called out, "1930," "1926," "1955." I could tell the teacher was mortified by these responses from the class. I answered, "I'll take any year from 1939 to 1945." My third question, "Name one year from the American Civil War." The class just stared at me, and then one pretty girl sitting right in front of me said, "That's easy; it was 1812." I turned facing the teacher and said, "A cheeseburger, coke and fries." Then a student with his head lying on his desk looked up and shouted out, "That happened before I was born." Embarrassed, the teacher just walked out of the room. Remember, these were present-day history students who were considered the best the school had to offer.

The point of all this is to show you how little the average person knows of history. Should they pop back in time and claim to be from the future, how little would they know about the time they were living in and the in-between time? So, if someone went back and said they were from the future, people would ask many questions, and the time traveler would be able to give very few answers. The "time traveler" would be considered a fraud, publicity-seeker, or even a psycho.

A time slip could happen to anyone, and we are not Doctors of History like the characters from *The Time Tunnel*. Let's face it, people tend to be more interested in watching gossip talk shows or engaging in computer games rather than watching news programs or historical documentaries. Fortunately, I learned from the people I interviewed who experienced a time slip that it did not last long. It is unsettling that we will never know those caught in a time slip who stayed at their destination permanently. From the lists of people worldwide who have simply vanished without a trace, could some be victims of this phenomenon?

THE HORROR OF TIME TRAVEL

Imagine a scenario where a person 60 years old in 2025 travels back fifty years to 1975 and arrives in the same town where they grew up. How would they react? They would only have the clothes on their back; whatever money they would have on them would be no good, and all identification they carried would be void. Any savings they may have had in 2025 has yet to happen, so they would be officially broke. If they tried to use the money they carried, they would risk arrest for passing counterfeit currency. That includes coins made after 1975.

If this happened to you, and you knew that your parents had died during those fifty years, could you resist the urge to visit them? Would you approach them and identify yourself as their son from the future? If somehow, they believed you, how would you handle their questions about their fate? During your talks, how would you handle watching yourself as a young child walking into the room? If this time slip didn't correct itself and you found yourself stuck there for even a few days, where would you eat and sleep?

Reading about time slips is one thing, but living one is a horror. Once you realize what happened, you will come to the sickening reality that you are truly alone. There is no one you can talk to about this. All the loved ones who were part of your life are gone. To sum it up, it would be as if you were waking up on another planet.

If your experience happens to take you back centuries ago, the problem will be even worse. When you find yourself so far in the past, you had better find a way to survive and do it quickly. After experiencing my time slip, I have spent many hours reflecting on how a person stuck in the past and truly alone, could exist. I came up with a possible solution to this complex and unique problem.

I discovered that a time slip brings you back to the exact location you were in. If you were on the corner of 42nd Street and 10th Avenue in New York City today and a time slip happened, you would be at the same intersection, just at another time. Finding yourself penniless, with no identification and no doubt wearing very odd clothing for the time, how would I approach this problem? After careful thought, I came up with a possible solution.

Avoiding Asylum Commitment

After my time slip, I wondered how to handle remaining permanently in the past. If I found myself in this predicament, what would I do? Who could I confide in, and whom could I trust? I had years to mull this over and to work out a detailed plan of how to exist in a world that had little in common with my life now.

You're probably wondering why I would write about being in a time slip that doesn't pop me back to my own time. It seems that everyone's account so far has been that they leave the present, appear in the past for a short time, and then reappear back where they started, in the present. I want to consider a more sinister possibility.

We are aware that people disappear all the time without a trace, and there are plenty of explanations why someone would. They may have run away with a large sum of money that wasn't theirs or blended into the crowd to escape being found by a jealous lover. Let's not leave out disappearing for political reasons or war crimes. After World War II, many Nazis disappeared. In time, a lot were found, and some weren't. I feel safe saying that a time slip disappearance wasn't a factor in these cases.

Let us not forget the high-profile disappearance of D.B. Cooper. In 1971, he boarded a flight with a powerful bomb in his briefcase. He demanded $200,000 in twenty-dollar bills and four parachutes from Northwest Orient Airlines. The aircraft landed, and they gave him the money and parachutes. He ordered them to resume the flight, he jumped out of the airplane and disappeared. No one ever heard from him again.

These examples all fit a pattern which does not shock us that the people involved suddenly vanished without a trace. What I am about to present to you is very odd, but much thought went into a plan to stay safe and navigate through the horrific dilemma of being caught in a time slip and never returning to the present.

Once you're convinced that your time slip is not passing, don't wait; you must begin your survival plan. Start by seeking out a church and telling the minister that you lost your memory but know you are a God-fearing man. Tell him that you're hungry and looking for work and lodging. The loss of memory is also an excuse to help cover what you don't know about the day-to-day use of tools, expressions, or customs of the period. It's the small things that a person of the future would not be aware of. If the minister feels pity for you, there is a good chance you may end up with room and board in return for working around the church. If this doesn't work at the first church, try another church and another until someone takes you in.

Whatever you do, don't go to the authorities. Even with the minister who has given you food and shelter, refrain from confiding your secret with him. You'd be asking for trouble and might end up in an insane asylum, which was the dumping ground for the mentally challenged in those earlier days.

During my research, I've encountered those who claimed to be from the past and/or the future. They were not taken seriously because their stories were unsubstantiated tales that echoed old sci-fi paperback novels of the 1950s. When I further investigated these reports, I found in many cases that the person submitting them was a fiction writer, having published numerous short stories or magazine articles.

Making these claims is the perfect way for someone to get attention. To illustrate this point, a schoolteacher told me she gave her class an assignment to write a short story. They were to work on it over the weekend and have it ready for submittal on Monday. She got stories from the old *Twilight Zone* and *The Outer Limits* TV shows of the 1960s. One of the students confessed to her that he did not think she ever saw these old black-and-white shows. So, someone trying to convince others that they are from the past or future could merely have been influenced by a vintage old black-and-white TV show or a dog-eared pulp fiction paperback from the '50s.

Today, we take psychiatry seriously, and reports from psychiatrists and psychologists differ from years ago. Now, detailed notes are taken during a session with a client; these notes may include audio recordings.

Sigmund Freud (b. 1856, d. 1939) is considered the father of modern psychology. Psychiatric studies using his technique started in the 20th century, which was not that long ago. Freud's theory suggests that human behavior is influenced by unconscious memories, thoughts, and urges and proposes that the psyche comprises three aspects: the id, ego, and superego.

Since those early days, we've introduced from Freud's initial theory various approaches to psychotherapy such as Behavior Therapy, which focuses on a person's behavior; Cognitive Therapy, which focuses on thoughts and assumptions; Humanistic Therapy, which is person and relationship-centered; and Integrative or Holistic Therapy, dealing with all aspects of a person's well-being, which may include alternative therapies like Reiki. Today, we look upon a person's mental health as a real thing and take it seriously.

Such an enlightened approach did not exist pre-1900s. If someone back then said he was from the distant past or future, there would be no question about it; the person would be considered insane and locked up. Keep in mind that no psychoanalyst existed back then. Any person with a mental problem would be on their own. No caretaker or doctor would find a need to record the ramblings of an insane person. Today, after an exhaustive search for medical records that date back over a hundred years of someone who talked about skipping time, I concluded that they don't exist. If there are such records, I couldn't find them.

But let us not jump ahead of ourselves; we need to go to the root of the subject. We need a basic understanding of the time slip phenomenon; what it is and is not.

The Media's Attempt at the Phenomenon

Television shows based on paranormal subjects have episodes that try to explain the time slip phenomenon, but I feel they fail in their attempt.

They focus on explaining time itself. For anyone who experiences a slip in time, the explanation or definition of time is not the issue. Every show resurrects Albert Einstein and his theory of traveling at the speed of light. I can't and won't challenge his theory that traveling at such speeds will affect a person's place in time.

Einstein calculates that the speed of light is 670,616,629 miles per hour. His theory of special relativity proposes that time is an illusion that moves relative to an observer. An observer traveling near the speed of light will experience time more slowly than a person at rest.

This is a very complex scenario, and a viewer of that TV show will be impressed by their scientific jargon, but unfortunately, it has nothing to do with a time slip. No one is traveling at the speed of light or taking a shortcut through a wormhole known for bending time and space. Yes, it's true that time is at the center of what we're discussing; however, I won't dedicate five chapters describing "time." I'm confident that those who are watching, listening, or reading about this phenomenon know what time is.

To illustrate my point, if I were to approach the sinking of the *Titanic* like those who produce today's paranormal shows, the time slip phenomenon would go like this: The *Titanic* was a ship traveling on the Atlantic Ocean, and it began its maiden voyage from England to its destination, New York. During its voyage, it inadvertently hit an iceberg, becoming badly damaged, and sank into the icy waters of the ocean in a few short hours. Once we establish those facts, the next forty-five minutes of the show would go into details of what water is, the buoyancy of objects, and the history of boats and ships over thousands of years. To add to their validity, they would produce experts in the field to confirm the nature of water.

Let's put experiencing time slips in its basic form. It's about some poor soul who finds themselves briefly projected back to a different time other than their own. Those questioned said the slip only lasted a few minutes before they returned to their time.

CONFUSION OF A TIME SLIP AND DISSOCIATION

While questioning those who have experienced a time slip, I ran into others who spoke about their loss of time, where they traveled great distances in a remarkably short time or even instantly. In psychology, this is called dissociation. This is not a time slip, nor should it be considered a paranormal event. A good definition would be an unaccountable lapse in time.

The first time I heard someone talk about this, I was in my early twenties. I worked for the Jones Motor Company, a trucking company based in Spring City, Pennsylvania. I worked for the Special Commodities Division. These are the trucks, or rigs, as they are called, with flatbed trailers hauling steel plates, large steel coils, and huge machines. Just about anything they were hauling had to be loaded with a crane. The tractors and trailers were owned by individuals and leased to the company.

Jones Motor Company was just one of the many companies with a division that hauled these special commodities. For the company, this worked out well because the maintenance of these tractors and trailers was the responsibility of the owners. The office I worked at was simply that—an office with a large parking lot. My office was on the second floor of a truck stop in South Kearny, New Jersey. There were no loading docks or forklifts, just an office with an adjoining room where the drivers sat waiting for a load of freight to be called in. A good portion of these drivers came from the East Coast, from Massachusetts to North Carolina. When these drivers entered the area, they would park their equipment in the lot, sign in, and wait for a load.

I had been working at the office for about six months when a driver walked into the drivers' room and said to all his fellow truckers, "I just crossed Pennsylvania in an hour." The drivers laughed and said he was nuts "because no one can do that." To travel the length of Pennsylvania would take at least four to five hours. I was watching all this from my desk and found it strange that the driver telling his story was visibly shaken up. As he recalled this story, he trembled and looked scared. At one point, I thought he would break out into tears. The other drivers continued to laugh, which caused the driver to leave the room after signing in. He remained sitting in his truck until he composed himself before returning to the drivers' room. This was just a happening that came and went, and I never thought about it again until during my time slip fact-finding for this book, I recalled this incident.

It wasn't long before I encountered a man with a similar story—my good friend, Anthony (Tony) Clemente, who is a master mechanic and whom I've known for years. Tony keeps my cars and my truck roadworthy. He's a fellow Freemason and Past Master of my Lodge, so he is considered my Masonic Brother. One day, while he was working on my truck, I mentioned my latest project, namely this book. His father, Tony Sr., was working in the garage and overheard my conversation. He came to me and wanted to tell his story of lost time. I looked into his eyes and saw the same fear as the driver I met years ago at the trucking company. Tony Sr. wiped his hands with a shop towel and told me his story.

Tony was a sailor in 1955 and was stationed in Norfolk, Virginia. Sailors who served on his ship would often vacation at nearby Virginia Beach. It was here in the summer of '55 that he met a beautiful woman. They immediately hit it off and continued a close bond through correspondence when his leave was over. This friendship quickly bloomed from a close relationship to an engagement and plans for marriage. She was living in Toledo, Ohio, and he was living in Belleville, New Jersey. When he had time, he would often venture to Ohio to see her.

Back in the 1950s, the roads weren't like the superhighways we have today. Reaching Toledo would take at least four hours of driving on the Ohio Turnpike. Unfortunately, his last trip there, on December 26, 1956, didn't end well. The question of religion was the stumbling point in their upcoming marriage. The couple couldn't resolve the problem and called off the marriage. Tony realized that this would be the last time he saw her.

That night, wanting to beat traffic and the forecasted inclement weather, he left her home at 10 p.m. Tony remembers heading for the Ohio Turnpike as it began to snow. He was handed his trip ticket from the toll booth when he approached the Ohio Turnpike. From his past trips, he knew that crossing Ohio was a four-hour trip and prepared himself for it. He claims that in what seemed like 5 minutes, he found himself facing the toll booth of the Pennsylvania Turnpike. He knew this was impossible! He was shocked. He pulled into the first service area in Pennsylvania to check out his car and contemplate what happened to him. There was no damage to the car, and he didn't get a speeding ticket from the police, so how did this happen?

When Tony recounted this story, he was convinced he crossed Ohio in five minutes. Yet, in reality, it took four hours, just as it normally does. Tony lost his memory of actually driving those four hours. In his heart, he crossed Ohio in five minutes. His story sounded just like the truck driver's I remembered years ago who claimed to have crossed Pennsylvania in an hour.

During Tony's four hours of driving, he must have obeyed the speed limit and stopped for fuel given the distances involved. He realized that the clock told him that four hours had passed, but he could not remember any of it. His body and mind were on autopilot as his thoughts were channeled somewhere else, most likely the loss of his love back in Toledo.

Tony Sr., is now in his 80s and continues to work as a mechanic with his son Tony Jr. This dissociation occurred over 60 years ago, yet to speak to him, you

Anthony Clemente, Sr. (L) Anthony Clemente, Jr.(R)
Photo by Karl Petry.

would think this happened yesterday. I have no doubt of his recall of the day of December 26, 1956.

When speaking to psychologists, I learned that this type of occurrence is not uncommon. Although some more serious disorders of dissociation would require psychiatric treatment, most of us have milder episodes at one time or another. If you think about it, you may remember an experience of driving home from work with your thoughts on other matters and arriving almost as if you were on autopilot. Just like a time slip, many who experience this type of event feel fear and often refuse to talk about it. But it's a common psychological phenomenon of dissociation.

It's understandable why dissociation and a time slip are often mistaken as the same. It is no reflection on the mental capabilities of these men. The truck driver probably drove his rig for many years before he retired, and Tony is still an active mechanic well into his eighties. If either the truck driver or the mechanic had mental issues, they wouldn't function so well in their day-to-day lives.

Retrocognition

Retrocognition is a displacement in time in which one sees into the past to either experience or review events of which one has no prior knowledge or to obtain accurate information that is not in one's memory. A time slip transports the person experiencing it to a point in the past. Retrocognition gives a glimpse of past events but leaves the person firmly in the present. When people speak about their time slip experience, they all share one thing in common—the location remains the same, but everything around them changes.

I never knew what retrocognition was or that I had it. I was a good friend of author Rosemary Ellen Guiley. She was a paranormal investigator who wrote over sixty books. She also authored encyclopedias that covered magic, ghosts and spirits, vampires, and witches, to name a few topics. She spent many days with Sue and me, and our conversations dealing with the paranormal would often begin after dinner and end around three in the morning. Sue couldn't keep up with our marathon chitchat sessions and would head for the sanctuary of the bedroom around ten.

Rosemary observed my ability on many occasions. We sometimes did a ghost investigation together, and she witnessed my retrocognition ability kick in. I was never conscious of what I was doing, but Rosemary watched me carefully, saw the results, and was impressed.

A couple of times when she was dating someone, and things seemed to be working out for her, she would make it a point to visit me. She wanted me to see her new beau and tell her if I saw something she should be aware of.

One example is when she called and said she met a nice religious guy and wanted my take on him. All she said was that he was from High Point, NC and left it at that. I never want anyone to give me details because they could be wrong, and that false information could mix up my thoughts. They pulled into the driveway about 1 p.m. They planned on staying for a few days, most likely to see some of the sights in New York City. I'm not far from the city, and you can see the city skyline from my house.

As we sat in the living room, my retrocognition gave me visions of the man. It sometimes felt like watching a television program, and sounds and dialogue often accompanied the visions.

Rosemary told the guy that I had this unusual ability and got the impression he brushed it off as nonsense. I was in the kitchen making a few drinks when Rosemary walked in. I quietly asked her if she knew that he was married. Looking shocked, she whispered back to me, "He said he was single." Then, carrying a tray of drinks and snacks, we both returned to the living room. I said to him, "You live in a large white house right off the highway." "Yes, I do," he answered. A short time later, I said, "You live in Albemarle," and he quickly said, "No, I live in High Point." It was obvious he was getting very nervous. He barely downed the drink before he excused himself, saying he had to make a few phone calls to his office, and headed for the guest room. Rosemary had told me before they made the trip, he had stopped by her apartment in Maryland and had dropped off a few things he didn't need to carry.

It wasn't long before he returned and said they weren't staying because of an emergency at work and would be leaving for Maryland immediately. I knew what started off as discomfort with me had now turned into a panic.

I got a call from Rosemary later that night. She said that when they returned to her apartment, he quickly grabbed an overnight bag and some dry cleaning he had in her closet, said goodbye, and left. When she went into the closet, she found a dry-cleaning receipt on the floor. The payment was billed to his wife's account with their home address in Albemarle.

Now, you should have an idea of what it's like to have the retrocognition ability. This also brings the time slip phenomenon into play. Could a time slip experience be linked to the phenomenon of retrocognition? My answer is no. They are totally different. Retrocognition happens spontaneously and takes the form of a vision. In my story of Rosemary's friend, I mentally saw images of the man's life and home and never felt that I was physically at his home in North Carolina.

Retrocognition and time slips share the same problem; academic standards can prove neither. To meet such standards, proof of time slips would require you to produce a time slip on demand in a specific experiment. The same applies to retrocognition; they'll want you to provide information on an event and time of their choosing, and any variation of the experiment would make the test void.

I once heard a parapsychologist give a lecture on ESP. The man was a professor at a well-known university in the Northeast who taught a course on parapsychology. He had a lab, and several of his students participated in the ESP research. A few of the students showed remarkable results during the testing. He approached the department head of the university and reported his findings.

The department wanted to do its own testing to ensure accurate results. So, they devised their own test and gave it to the students involved. Their test proved these particular students had a higher degree of accuracy. Not satisfied, they redesigned another test and tried it again. The results once again proved the students involved had ESP greater than the norm. Not satisfied with those results, they redesigned the test again. This time, the test was so complicated and confusing for the participants that the results showed no higher ESP ability than normal. This final test satisfied them.

When recalling this event, the professor was very upset and claimed the department heads' minds were already made up, and they would do whatever they needed to do to ensure his ESP tests would fail. He later learned that the university was worried that if the financial donors knew the money that they provided to the university was being spent on studies in the paranormal field, they would withhold future contributions. They made it a point to derail all parapsychology and ESP studies.

On a positive note, retrocognition has been used successfully in psychic criminology to solve crimes and find missing persons. Adding to the mystique of retrocognition, psychologist Gardner Murphy had a theory that many sightings of ghosts and apparitions could be retrocognition. It was his belief that a person, for a moment, becomes momentarily displaced in time, and the individual is not actually transported back in time but remains in the present while hallucinating the scenes from the past. You can see there are plenty of suggestions pointing to a strong case of retrocognition throughout the psychic world.

Do we agree with Dr. Gardner Murphy that a time slip could be retrocognition and the person experiencing this phenomenon is hallucinating? I must disagree. The problem I have with the doctor's explanation is that he assumes that all time slips are hallucinations. Sometimes, it may be a hallucination; however, not always. He does not account for the descriptions of very real phenomena as in the many cases I describe. Retrocognition is a displacement in time in which one apparently sees into the past, to either experience or review events of which one has no prior knowledge, or to obtain accurate information which is not in one's own memory.

Most Notable Time Slip Story

If you never heard of a time slip and were experiencing one, you would swear the images you saw were ghosts. "There is no doubt about it: they are ghosts, period!"

One report of what we call today a time slip dates to 1901. Eleanor Jourdain and Ann Mobely were British women visiting the Palace of Versailles in France. The Palace was a huge tourist attraction, just as it is today, and a "must-see" site when in the area.

The Palace has 2300 rooms. That is no typo, 2300 rooms. That would include Marie-Antoinette's personal Chamber, The Hall of Mirrors, The King's Private Apartments, and a multitude of Galleries spread throughout the building, and the list of rooms goes on and on.

After these two women completed their tour of the Palace, they wanted to see the two-story chapel, Petit Trianon. It was built in the mid-1700s by architect Ange-Jacques Gabriel and was one of Marie Antoinette's favorite places on the grounds.

As these two women were making their way to the chapel, Eleanor described "a heavy dreaminess" atmosphere, and both were experiencing feelings of depression and loneliness.

In addition to the awkward feelings they felt, they saw men and women dressed in 18th-century garb. Eleanor and Ann noted that one of the men wearing a heavy black cloak showed facial scaring usually caused by smallpox.

Anyone who actually had a time slip shares a common trait: They are scared and will not immediately speak about it. Such was the case with Eleanor and Ann. A week later, they shared their saga, recalling their story at the Palace, and were convinced what they saw were ghosts. It was 1901, and the concept of a time slip was unknown.

Could they have been right that what they saw were ghosts? No, I will stick with my time slip scenario because of what happened to Eleanor and Ann when they returned to the Palace in 1904. Wanting to retrace their steps leading up to their ghostly encounter, they could no longer find the trail around the Palace they used on their last visit. Many of the landmarks they recalled seeing: a cottage, a grotto, and a small bridge that spanned over a ravine, weren't there anymore.

Confused about the disappearance of these places the women studied a map of the Palace grounds drawn in 1780. This older map clearly indicated the missing structures and the Palace grounds as they had seen it.

This bit of information should clarify the question of ghosts vs. time slips. If you happen to see a ghost, the area around the ghostly image doesn't change, but in a time slip, it does.

It Can't Be Possible; Somebody Is Just Making This Up

The thought of a time slip sounds unbelievable, but as to be expected, today's science experts say without a doubt that the phenomenon does not exist.

This is not the first time experts have come forward to challenge an eyewitness' story. For years, seamen described a terrifying happening at sea: giant waves towering over their ships. As a result, some ships suffered extreme damage, while other ships sank. The experts of the time called "monster" waves impossible and questioned the sanity of the seamen who dreamed up their giant wave story.

Stories of these giant waves were considered folklore and passed on from generation to generation. I'm sure there were times when a grandpa, a former seaman, sat down with his family and recounted his near-death experience with one of these mythical waves. His family just smiled and passed the word amongst the children to let Grandpa tell his story and act as if it was real. The assumption was that it could not be true because the educated experts said so.

For hundreds of years, this went on. To protect themselves from ridicule, a seaman had to refrain from commenting on any of these wave encounters or risk ridicule from the unbelieving public.

It wasn't until January 1, 1995, that the existence of these monster waves was confirmed. A laser detector on the Draupner oil-drilling platform, owned by Statoil and located 100 miles off the coast of Norway, recorded the event.

Suddenly, not only do we believe in these waves, but our scientific experts now have all the information on how these giant waves come about. I should add that they are the ones who came up with the term "Rogue Waves." If I asked these wave experts why they once denied the existence of rogue waves, they would say I was mistaken and would act as if they had always believed in them. I find it strange that all those once nay-sayer experts disappeared after the oil drilling platform recorded one on January 1, 1995.

Our rogue wave experts have now gone on to explain the many unsolved mysteries of the waters, attributing many to these killer waves. Even now, some experts claim it was a rogue wave that sunk the *Edmond Fitzgerald* in Lake Superior in November of 1975. The abundance of video cameras accessible by ship's passengers and crew, recording their encounters with these waves, including cruise ships, makes their case more acceptable to the public and their academic peers. What are the chances that at least one of these wave experts will apologize to seaman Grandpa for not believing his giant wave stories?

Will time slips go the way of rogue waves? I can hear today's experts saying, "It's not true; it can't be true," until someone uncovers why it happens. Then you'll see experts come out of the woodwork insisting they knew about time slips all along.

Light, Chemicals, Paper & Celluloid

Let's look at time slips in a different way. Time slips are much like photography. What is photography? In its early form, the basic premise was to record an image on a metal plate, or later, through development, metal plates were replaced by paper. What was captured on the metal or paper medium will not change and will exist, for as long as the photograph exists.

Joseph Nicephore Niece produced the earliest photograph in 1827. I wonder what people thought of him when he shared his idea of photography with his family and friends. The argument Joseph Niece must have heard was that we have some wonderful artists who can take a person's image or a scene and transfer it onto a canvas in oil or watercolor paint. What could be better than that? Through his experimentation, Joseph Niece made a camera known as Obscura, a crude box without a lens. He carried it to his window, aimed it, and took an image of the street below. That photograph, created almost two hundred years ago, still exists today!

Society, not satisfied with the static image, developed a way to make the images move. This involved taking a series of photographs on a medium called celluloid and connecting them in series, processing those photos, and then putting them on a roll. The next step was to project a strong light behind the roll while it was being unreeled. Those images took on life, and now they moved. It was what we called a motion picture.

The first motion picture was shot in 1888. It was a 2.11-second film called *The Roundhay Garden Scene*. Louis Le Prince produced it and showed four people walking in a garden. By 1902, the film industry had graduated to making full-length films such as *A Trip to the Moon* (1902) and *The Great Train Robbery* (1903). Unlike a stage play, people could now see these performances on film again and again, thanks to this new medium of motion pictures.

These film images were in black and white and would be for many years until future technology would make a breakthrough in the development of color. Early efforts to make black-and-white films color was a crude process and very expensive due to the tremendous labor needed to color each frame by hand. When the film was finished, at best, the result was a smeary imagery in blurry color.

The next evolution in filmmaking happened on October 6, 1927, when the first sound film, *The Jazz Singer*, premiered. It had both a voice soundtrack for dialogue and a track for music. As everyone would expect, the audience loved it, and the motion picture companies abandoned the making of silent films. With all their efforts, we were now in the making of "talkies." By the late 1920s, we had two-dimensional moving images capable of sound.

By this time, you are wondering about the connection between a time slip and the subject of photography and motion pictures. There is a connection. If we showed someone from the eighteenth century the image of a recorded person, projected on a wall, talking or singing, what would they believe was happening? The thought of a person not being there would never enter their mind. I doubt if you explained the technology involved with film, recording, and projecting that they would comprehend the technology involved. In their minds, sorcery and magic would prevail over technology. I left out television because the content of the shows, especially the commercials, would completely blow their minds.

Could a time slip be some kind of projection from the past? *One interesting element is that no one I interviewed ever physically touched a person from their time slip.*

Visually, we have advanced to making three-dimensional images called holograms. In a relatively short time, technology has enabled us to interact with advanced holograms. Most notably, to teach future generations of the horrors of Nazi Germany, a real holocaust survivor was recorded in a full body image, sitting on a chair, facing the audience, telling his day-by-day account of being incarcerated in a Nazi concentration camp in Europe back in the 1940s. The holocaust survivor featured in the hologram is Erin Elser, and the exhibit is at the Illinois Holocaust Museum and Educational Center in Chicago. The hologram not only made the image three-dimensional but was also interactive and programmed to answer questions asked by the audience. For all intents and purposes, the hologram gave the impression to the audience of being a real person sitting in front of them.

Could a time slip be a natural holographic image projected at random to various worldwide locations? This could be a relatively common occurrence throughout the world, but unless someone is there to see it, this phenomenon goes unnoticed.

When I experienced my time slip, I felt as if I was transported to another time. Everything seemed real, from the ground under my feet to the smell of the air and the breeze of the wind. Could it be I was dropped in an active, immense super hologram that took up a large geographic area? I call it a hologram because it is the closest reference we have today that I can think of. However, maybe it is something like a hologram but different. Unfortunately, we are searching for an explanation based solely on our understanding of our reality today.

There is no reason to believe that time slips don't appear on a regular basis. Could we be sharing our time with that of the past, only in a different dimension? Is there a place where time slips happen on a regular basis?

Time Slips vs. Time Travel

Too often, when we speak of time slips, they are automatically categorized as the same as time travel. In short, they are not. The belief is that in time travel, a person has some degree of control in traveling through time. They can select the place and the year where they want to go, whereas a time slip happens unannounced and occurs at the place where the person happens to be. They have no control over the time or a place other than where they happen to be standing. The time could be fifty or three hundred years, and they're totally at the mercy of where the phenomenon takes them.

Ships and Trains Skipping
Through Time

Seamen have told stories throughout the years of seeing old sailing ships while they were on their voyage. They would see a ship, and then a short time later, it would disappear. Sailors called them ghost ships for lack of a better term. One explanation is that what they saw was nothing more than a ship experiencing a time slip.

I'm aware of the ghost stories of ships lost in the oceans, such as the *Flying Dutchman*, *Mary Celeste*, *USS Porpoise*, and the *Cyclops*. Not limited to the oceans, let's not forget ghost ships of the Great Lakes like the *SS Bannockburn* or the *Cornelia B. Windiate*, and many mentioned these experiences taking place in the Bermuda Triangle, the areas within the three points of Miami, Bermuda, and Puerto Rico, where strange disappearances happened to ships and airplanes. Could some of these ghost ships have appeared or disappeared through a time slip?

People are fascinated by ghost stories, and one that keeps surfacing is about the train station in Newark, NJ. It's said that on the 10th of each month, around midnight, people hear a train passing on the tracks of Newark Penn Station. This event is not limited to a handful of people, but hundreds. Some see an old, coal-burning, vintage train passing on the tracks. Don't be so quick to discount this as some mass hallucination because a similar thing occurred only a few miles from Newark.

On February 16th, 2024, I lectured at the Wyckoff Masonic Lodge in Ramsey, New Jersey. This was my first opportunity to talk to an audience who had never heard of time slips. At one point, I told the story of old trains suddenly appearing at the Newark train station. I caught one of the audience attendees looking surprised. Toward the end of my talk, I asked if there were any questions. The man, Joseph Rodrigues, recalled his train story and told the crowd.

Joseph Rodrigues was the owner of the Village Construction Company. On December 10th, 2012, his construction company was hired to restore the Bellevue Avenue train station in Upper Montclair, NJ. Because they were working on or around the tracks that were active, they were aware of the time that the commuter trains would pass on the tracks, giving them the time to remove all personal items and equipment off the tracks.

A few hours before the commuter train was scheduled to pass, Joe asked Mario, one of his workers, to get a jackhammer and bring it to the site so they could smash through a concrete wall. When Mario arrived with the jack hammer, he was thrilled to tell Joe about the antique train he saw that went by. He said he heard an odd-sounding whistle different from the trains he was used to. Joe, of course, said that no train had passed. They couldn't because the tracks were full of workers and equipment. Mario insisted that what he saw was real but could not explain why the train disappeared so quickly after it passed.

The time slip possibility I brought up seemed to be a viable answer to the question that had remained on Joe's mind for many years.

Village Construction Company photo of Bellevue Train Station in Montclair, NJ circa 2012. Photo by Joe Rodrigues.

Fascination With Time Travel

As I mentioned before, a time slip and time travel are not the same. Say "time slip," and the response from everyone is that you are a time traveler. Can't help it because it's impossible for the public to sort out the two. We will make comparisons of both throughout this book. A time slip is a method of traveling backward in time, but impossible for us to control.

Nikola Tesla believed that time and space could be influenced by using strong rotating magnetic fields. He first came up with this idea back in 1895 while he was researching his step-up transformer. He was convinced that by using a combination of high-voltage electricity and magnetic fields, a doorway would appear, and it would allow us to enter other times.

Knowing what we know of Mr. Tesla, I'm sure his intended goal in time travel was to enable individuals to be physically transported, using his device, to a pre-selected time and place.

Many stories surrounded Tesla's theories, and scientists and inventors dealt with and experimented with his use of electrical fields. When he died on January 7th, 1943, in his room on the 33rd floor of the Roosevelt Hotel in New York City, all his papers, books, and belongings disappeared. It's been said that our government was responsible for the removal. I could not find any evidence to support that; however, what happened to all his written notes and papers regarding his projects and theories? We'll never know; no one is talking. Over the years, when asked about it, there has been a total denial of government involvement, and no one from the private sector will acknowledge the event.

As mentioned previously, Nikola Tesla was known for his research using strong magnetic fields. Later, in 1943 (eight months after Tesla's death), the United States, using this premise, conducted a top-secret experiment that, if successful, would make warships invisible to radar. They took Tesla's strong magnetic field generator and mounted the device onto a World War II Cannon-class destroyer escort named the *USS Eldridge*. On October 28, 1943, the test took place while anchored at the Philadelphia Shipyard.

Witnesses said the ship had a strange greenish-blue glow around it and then suddenly disappeared. The vessel was reported to have appeared at the Norfolk Naval Shipyard in Virginia, then disappeared and reappeared at the Philadelphia Shipyard. This could be classified as a rare man-made time slip and a time travel episode. Experiments of this nature continued during and after World War II. Unsurprisingly, the government denies conducting such experiments before, during, or after the war. The government's official position was that the Philadelphia Experiment was nothing more than a fabricated story, rejecting all eyewitness reports and written records to the contrary.

To this day, if you mention weird experiments dealing with time slips or time travel, don't be surprised to hear of the experiments taking place at Fort Hero, also known as the Montauk Project, located at Montauk Point, Long Island, New York. When investigating the Montauk Project, it's difficult to sort out what really happened there and what was fictitious, or what misinformation the government spread about this place to cover their tracks, should these stories be real. One such story surfaced on the experimental use of LSD on adults and children; another was the government's intense experiments in time travel. A photograph has surfaced showing an actual time travel chair in one of the rooms. I don't believe any government would invest a tremendous amount of its resources into a theory if there wasn't a chance of it working.

Remote Viewing

We mentioned the desire for an understanding and possible use of time slips and time travel, starting with Tesla's research on the subject and the government's attempt to make this theory a reality. I always say, if you have an ability to do something that few or no one can do, this ability is deemed worthless unless it can put money in someone's pocket.

In our high-tech world, every country's military tries to get the edge over their competition. What could be better than having a non-electronic, non-mechanical device that can accomplish the impossible? How about someone who can remotely spy on the competition without leaving the room? Such was the program that the US Central Intelligence Agency started in 1972.

They called the program Remote Viewing (RV). The objective was to see if RV could be used in military espionage.

The CIA's program was called the Stargate Project. Over time, although it wasn't as accurate as they would have liked in its military goals, the program still had promise and could have been used in other areas. But for now, its usefulness was over. Funding stopped, and the entire RV project was scrapped. In its wake, there were RV superstars such as Joseph McMoneagle, Russell Targ, Harold Puthoff, and Ingo Swann, pioneers in this new field who were now unceremoniously pushed aside. I'm not implying that present-day Remote Viewing doesn't exist or that some government factions aren't using it. If they are, they're keeping it under wraps.

We're back to what I always say, if there is no way to benefit from the investigation of the time slip phenomena, why bother?

THE TIME SLIP DOESN'T END
WHEN YOUR TIME SLIP ENDS

It's been years since my time slip experience. After all the time that has passed, you would expect the experience to fade away. Why not? Many people have trouble remembering some of their classmates' names or trying to pinpoint the exact date when something significant happened to them. Whenever I interviewed a person who had a time slip, they remembered to the minute detail what happened before, during, and after the event. The passing of years has no effect on their time slip memory; they have a total recollection of that day, remaining steadfast in their recall.

Often, when I'm alone or trying to sleep, memories of my time slip episode will return. Even in a dream state, recalling the faces and expressions of the long-gone people I encountered is terrifying. When I remember the sound of their voices, talking amongst each other about this strange-looking and oddly dressed uninvited visitor that just showed up, it adds a heightened degree of horror to the memory of the slip.

In my heart, I realize that I could never be a part of their world, whether it be for five minutes or five years. I can't shake the thought that everyone I was interacting with had been dead for over 200 years. If I were to mix with them, possessing the knowledge of 200 years in the future, knowing their fate and the generations to follow, I would be considered a God or a Demon.

If my time slip didn't happen, the concept of momentarily slipping back in time, even for a few minutes, would mean nothing more to me than a low-budget B-movie script.

Everything Points to Liverpool

One place is always mentioned when the subject of time slips comes up: Bold Street in the city of Liverpool, England. People experience the phenomenon more often there than anywhere else in the world. With this in mind, I had to take a trip to Liverpool to see firsthand what Bold Street was all about.

Before my trip, I was in contact with Peter Crawley of the paranormal investigative group Ghost Quest, which is connected with The Association for the Scientific Study of Anomalous Phenomena. We were to meet at the hotel the day before we investigated Bold Street. My good friends, who live in the UK, respected psychic mediums Dean and Stuart James Foy, along with my wife, psychologist Dr. Sueli, were my investigative team.

The time slip phenomenon does not happen on demand, so the chance of something happening while I was there would be a million to one. Yet, I had to see if I had any feelings about the street or if strange visions would appear to me, consciously or subconsciously. The trip was set, and soon, we were on our way.

My wife, Sueli, and I departed from New Jersey's Newark Airport, which is also known as Newark Liberty. We would land in Dublin, Ireland, go through customs, and then board another flight to Birmingham, England. Birmingham is close to Dean and Stuart's home, so this airport is ideal for us. The flight was long, the dinner and snacks they served were good, and I got to see the latest Godzilla vs. Kong film. Our connection for Birmingham was flawless and landed on time. After we retrieved our luggage, I heard Stuart's voice calling out our names. Within minutes we were on our way.

It was early in the morning, so after leaving the airport, we went to an all-you-can-eat breakfast buffet. The pub had all the English had to offer in the way of breakfasts: sausages, a.k.a. "bangers," bacon, baked beans, eggs, black pudding, waffles, pizza, toast, spicy hash brown potatoes, fried bread and biscuits with gravy, topping off the meal with various desserts, coffee, tea, or soda. Welcome to the UK!

The next morning, we got up early and enjoyed Stuart's delicious homemade English breakfast and waited for morning rush hour traffic to pass before we started our trip to Liverpool. We loaded up Stuart and Dean's Vauxhall with our luggage and made our way to the M6 motorway. We had reservations at the Liner Hotel, with check-in at 3 p.m. Peter Crawley, the UK paranormal investigator, was to meet us there.

The traffic on the M6 was extremely heavy, adding an hour to the trip. Because of our delay, we didn't make it to the hotel until almost 4 p.m. In my previous texts to him, I asked Peter to meet us at the hotel at 3.

I had never met Peter, and I had no idea what he looked like. As the four of us entered the hotel with our luggage, we noticed a man standing in front of the hotel's entrance looking at the people walking by. Sueli said to me, "That's probably Peter." She left the hotel

(L to R) Peter Crawley, Stuart and Dean James Foy.
Photo by Karl Petry.

and confirmed it was Peter. After checking in, we had dinner at the hotel's dining room. Poor Peter was hit with a barrage of questions from all of us. He gave us detailed information about Bold Street and shared one account that stood out amongst the many other stories. Peter's input helped us plan for the next day.

CRAWLEY'S REPORT

Peter didn't have any personal experiences with time slips but shared the most memorable stories from Bold Street. He talked about an incident in 1996 when a couple, Frank and Carol, went shopping. Carol wanted to buy a book at Waterstones bookstore, a huge store on Bold Street. On the way, Frank met an old friend and conversed with him on the street while Carol continued to the bookstore, where she was to meet up with Frank later.

After Frank left his friend, he continued to Bold Street and headed for Waterstones; however, when he approached the store, he saw the name Cripps above the door. Confused, he took a step back, and a van beeping his horn passed him with the name Cardin's on its side.

Something was wrong; all the cars on the street were no longer from 1996 but dated back to the late 1940s and '50s. The people on the street were dressed in the same style.

Frank was confused and worried. He headed for the store entrance, and as he got closer, he noticed items on display in the store windows were products such as umbrellas, shoes, and handbags from the '40s and '50s. He also saw a woman named Julie, totally perplexed, looking up at the store's sign and wearing modern-day clothing. Seeing Frank, she stood there waiting for him. Frank went into the shop, followed by Julie, where suddenly the building turned once again into a bookstore.

Frank was a former police officer, trained to remember facts and not easily swayed into believing that what he saw and experienced was due to a paranormal happening. This makes Frank an excellent time slip witness and adds credibility to his experience. Peter also told me that Frank and Julie remain friends to this day. Cardin, the name on the van with the beeping horn, was later identified as a store that dated back to the '50s.

Thief Escapes Through Time

In 2006, a store security guard pursued a shoplifter named Sean down various streets in Liverpool. Now on Hanover Street, Sean paused, exhausted, and felt that his surroundings seemed oddly different.

While recovering from exhaustion, he hid and waited for the guard to pass him. But the guard never came. Sean resumed walking down Hanover

Street, crossing over to Bold Street. But something was radically wrong. The people he encountered and the cars he saw were from decades past. It did not take long before panic set in. Sean knew that he had somehow slipped back in time. He checked his cellphone, but it did not work. Sean then walked toward a newspaper stand and glanced at the *Daily Post*. The date on the newspaper was May 18, 1967.

He was afraid, and like all those who experienced their own time slip, he wondered what would happen if he didn't return to the present time. What would all the people he knew think happened to him? These thoughts and looking into the faces of the people around him, all from 1967, scared him terribly. Miraculously, he suddenly returned to modern day 2006.

He was later interviewed by a local newspaper and gave the same account of his time slip multiple times. The Security Guard, when questioned, stated that Sean ran into a dead-end alley and disappeared.

These are only a few stories often told about the Bold Street time slips. How many are never told?

ARRIVING ON BOLD STREET

The following afternoon, we arrived on a rainy Bold Street. The street is blocked from vehicular traffic for most of the day and open to motorized vehicles only when the stores and restaurants need to be restocked. Bold Street is about four blocks long.

A view of Bold Street. Photo by Karl Petry.

At the top of the street is the Church of St. Luke. To the locals, it is known as the "bombed-out church" because it still shows the scars from the bombing that happened to it during World War II. Many cafés and small stores line the street. People would crisscross the street, bouncing from side to side, ducking into these small stores for food, drink, or whatever struck their fancy.

I hoped to sense some kind of energy emitting from the street, but I didn't. That's not surprising; with the thousands of people who walk on this street daily, only a few, on rare occasions, would experience this phenomenon.

However, following Peter's story about Frank and Carol, I made my way to where this astounding time slip occurred.

It was raining as our group headed down Bold Street. On this May Day, when you would expect people to dress in lightweight shirts, those around me wore jackets with hoodies instead. Of course, me being Mr. USA, stood out as the odd one on the street, wearing a thin shirt with no head covering. The folks on the street stayed close to the buildings to avoid the constant rain as best they could. I tucked my camera under my shirt to protect my camera lens from fogging and rain droplets, which would ruin my photos. I finally reached my destination, 14 Bold Street, the Frank and Carol Time Slip incident spot.

Being a person who is sensitive to paranormal sensations, I didn't sense any extraneous power emitting from the street or buildings. When a time slip happens, it could be just like a light switch; either it's on or it's off.

Bold Street is located above the city's underground rail network, and some have speculated that the electronics and power beneath finds its way to the street, causing hallucinations for the people walking above it. If that were true, the leakage of that magnitude would be substantial and would be detected. I'm sure if that were the case, the city of Liverpool would want to put a stop to it. By comparison, the New York City subway has 472 stations and covers over 665 miles (1070 km) of track. With all this, the trains, tracks, and power, to my knowledge, no street in New York City has reported incidents of time slips like that of Liverpool's Bold Street.

The Haute Dolci Restaurant at 14 Bold Street as it is today. In 1996, at this location was Dillons Book Store. The time slip brought it back to the late 1940s or early 1950s.
Photo by Karl Petry.

Can't Go to Liverpool Without Visiting the Home of The Beatles

I am a Beatles fan, plain and simple. Here I was in the hometown of these lads, and I wasn't going to miss the chance to see where John, Paul, George, and Ringo grew up. We arranged to take a private Beatles tour in Liverpool. There are many tours available; some have brightly colored buses while others are more on the personal size. We chose the more intimate personal tour offered by *Liverpool Beatles Tours*. Who knows when I'll ever have another chance to visit Liverpool, so I thought I might as well take advantage of the situation and go first class.

Right on time, a large Mercedes limo met us at the hotel's front door. That's where we met Ian, our chauffeur and tour guide. The first stops were at the childhood homes of each of the band members. I was surprised to see how small the houses were and that they were attached to other homes that all looked the same (row houses), with two rooms upstairs and two rooms downstairs. "Two-up Two-down" is the term they use to describe these buildings. A short distance away, we made our way to Penny Lane. Now I can put a place to the name and song.

What shocked me was the number of tour companies at the various Beatles locations we went to. At each stop, we bumped into many other tours that visited the same locations. I kept thinking that this group that disbanded more than half a century ago still attracted people who love their music and were interested in their personal lives and where they grew up.

It rained the entire time we were in England, and for a brief moment, the rain turned into a heavy mist as we visited St. Peter's Church graveyard on Church Road. This mist gave the experience a special eeriness, befitting the circumstances. In the graveyard behind the church lay the remains of Eleanor Rigby. This was the grave that inspired the Beatles' song of the same name.

It was here, back on July 6, 1957, in the field just beyond the graveyard, they had an outing for the neighborhood that included sideshows, ice cream, lemonade, and the skiffle group, The Quarrymen, for musical entertainment. John Lennon was a member of The Quarrymen, and that was the day he met Paul McCartney for the first time.

If ever I wanted to experience a time slip, it would be at this 1957 event, but of course, it didn't happen. We made our way to Strawberry Fields, now a tourist stop, for refreshments and Beatles memorabilia. Having our fill of tea, coffee, and scones, we proceeded to the home of Brian Epstein, the Beatles' first manager. We topped off the tour with a stop at The Cavern Club, where we saw a full-size bronze statue of John Lennon leaning against the wall. Our Beatles tour was fantastic.

A final note about our Beatles tour; Ian, our limo driver, was under the impression that we came from the United States just for the tour, but while he was taking us to Strawberry Fields for some refreshments, I told him the purpose for our visit to Liverpool was to investigate time slips. Ian had never heard of time slips, but as we returned to the limo, we could all see him on his phone. He was looking up time slips in Liverpool! You know he'll be mentioning the time slip phenomena of Liverpool on all his future tours.

Bronze John Lennon statue facing the entrance of the Cavern Club. Photo by Karl Petry.

TIME SLIPS REPORTED AT THE ROLLRIGHT STONES

While we were in the UK, Stuart and Dean suggested that we visit the Rollright Stones. They make it a point to visit the site a few times a year and told us that there is something mystical about the site.

It's located near the village of Long Compton, on the border of Oxfordshire and Warwickshire. Once there, you'll find three Neolithic and Bronze Age monuments near the village of Long Compton.

Over the years, people have come from all over the UK and around the world to visit this site. For many, it is a pilgrimage. Visitors carry out varying activities depending on their reason for coming. Some, who hold

Wiccan or pagan beliefs, may perform rituals, walking clockwise/sunwise (deosil) to manifest something, or to cast a magical circle. If they walk counterclockwise (widdershins), they are usually banishing something; it could be a negative influence in their life, or something as simple as a desire to lose weight. Other practitioners enjoy blending with the energy of the place and communing with the spirits of the sacred site.

On another level, visitors who are curious or simply enjoy heritage sites try to count the stones. Oddly, one may count the stones many times and never get the same number twice.

When you visit the Rollright Stones, expect to see people touching the stones and leaning against them, hoping that by just being there, they will bring some healing power to their lives. We went to the Rollright Stones on this trip because there have been reports that people have experienced time slips there.

We arrived mid-afternoon, parking our car on the side of the road. There are no designated areas for parking; it remains a wooded, tree-lined roadway, and one must know where the Rollright Stones are. They have an honor box and a sign requesting a donation of two pounds for entry. The day we arrived a car was on the field with a couple next to a handwritten sign stating the entry fee. Either the admission box was defective, or an enterprising couple found a way to subsidize their income.

Throughout the years, teams of scientists, students, surveyors, and even dowsers from around the world have made their way to this site equipped with scientific gear to find any anomalies.

While conducting their investigative research, they reported a few incidents where their personnel witnessed items like automobiles vanishing, strange animals appearing and disappearing, and even old-fashioned horse-drawn wagons appearing on the road, then suddenly fading away. Like most scientists, they had their theories of what they encountered. What they didn't rule out is that their witnesses had each experienced the time slip phenomenon.

Eternalism has the view that all points in time are equally real.

Three Neolithic limestones from The Rollright Stones.
Photo by Karl Petry.

WHY DO PEOPLE KEEP THEIR TIME SLIP A SECRET?

A person faces a conundrum when they experience a time slip. For starters, they fear telling anyone because they know the reaction they can expect from their audience. The public fails to understand that an actual time slip is not a psychological meltdown. It is not a hallucination and certainly not the result of the idiotic phrase I often hear, "Maybe it's something you ate." It's not a vision. It is an actual physical transference of matter from the now to the then.

How else to explain how two or more people experience the same time slip? What people can't get their heads around is that this is not like ghost hunting.

If a house is reported to be haunted, the investigators will inspect the premises, and if nothing happens, they will return again and again. These paranormal investigators have isolated the place of the ghostly anomalies and will choose the method and gear to carry out their investigation. On the other hand, a time slip is a random occurrence. No one knows when or where it will happen. Although Bold Street in Liverpool is a hot spot for time slips, no one knows when or where the next one will happen on that street.

Here is food for thought: maybe time slips happen on Bold Street at odd hours when the street is empty. Since these events last only a short time, there is no one there to witness the event or say how many times or where on the street it happens. Victims of time slips report it is happening during daylight hours; does that mean it doesn't happen at night?

It's a matter of how we approach time slips. This is a paranormal event and should be handled as such. The public wants to approach it as if it is a normal event. Since it isn't, they're upset, and if they don't get the answers they want when they want them, they'll simply dismiss the whole thing.

Over the years, odd things were recorded from photos, movie film, digital photographs, and video, and the responses range from, "I'm not sure what it is," or "It could be photoshopped." No one will stick their neck out and say that the event is truly paranormal and must be treated as such. When I meet paranormal investigators, and they show me their latest gadgetry for recording ghostly images or sounds to prove their findings, I ask them, why bother? With the technology we have today, anything could be photoshopped. So any evidence you show them, no matter how true or pure it is, they'll disregard. Many of these critics have taken the stance, "No one can fool me!" Once they say that, they'll usually end with the comment, "I'm aware of all the tricks out there, and when I see something that's real, I'll tell you."

During its wide-scale use, why didn't the public know of the subliminal messages being used in films and television shows? This was an advertising technique used to increase sales. For example, in movie theaters, the image of a hot dog was spliced into a film for a fraction of a second. Although not seen by the audience, this tactic had the effect of a dramatic jump in hot dog sales during the intermission. When asked, no one saw the hot dog on the screen, but their brain picked it up. This subliminal incentive to boost sales is illegal now, but we know it worked when it was used.

Regarding our original question, why do people keep their time slips a secret? Because no one wants to be confronted with those who will laugh and mock them. It hurts even if it's only a few who act this way.

If you bring up the subject at a gathering, stand back for the bombardment of silly questions and theories from your audience. The person sharing their time slip event does not appreciate others taking their experience as a joke. Their encounter is serious, and there's no place for levity.

There is a pattern to people's time slip experiences. They start off by saying how scared they were when it was happening. Once they realized they were taken suddenly into the past, they feared never returning to their present time and seeing their loved ones again. While the time slip was happening, they were confused, trying to figure out what was happening to them. Just when they wanted to believe it was just a dream, things suddenly worsened, and they found themselves interacting with people from the past.

Interaction could be the simple act of the person turning their head in the direction of the people or hearing their voices directed at them. This should be confirmation that they are not dreaming. This interaction with "slip" people from the past, which seems like a minor event, has now brought the experiencer from fear to sheer terror. When the time slip ended and they were returned to their normal time, they wanted to escape the area as fast as possible and put it all behind them.

Now that they have experienced this phenomenon, what do they do next? The people I interviewed were reluctant to tell family and friends of the abnormal trek they took in time. I didn't speak about my event for over a year, and others I questioned refused to tell anyone about theirs for an equally long time.

In time, the word may come out about your fantastic journey. Pseudo-intellectuals will try to impress their friends by asking you what sounds like informative, important questions, but they're not. You can expect the opening salvo of questions to go like this: "When did this happen? What time of the day was it? Was there a full moon that day? What was the weather like? What was the temperature like? How about sun flares? What did you eat before this happened? Did this ever happen to anyone else in your family? Do you sleep well at night? Were you under any emotional strain at that time? How is your overall health?" I saved the best for last: "Are you a Christian?" and "Do you believe in God?" Then, to show compassion toward you, they'll end with, "Maybe you should see a psychologist or psychiatrist. I'm sure they can help you."

After hearing your story, you will find many never actually heard what you said. What they heard or thought they heard, is that your time slip was going back in time for a period you could control. I know this sounds ridiculous, but this was a common reaction from those hearing about someone's time slip. As I mentioned before, it is difficult for many to separate a time slip from time travel. When you insist that what happened was a non-planned flash that removed you from today to a time in the past, you'll realize you are raining on their parade.

You are preventing them from enlightening you on how to use your time travel to amass riches. "I would buy gold that was cheap back then, and when I returned, it would be worth a fortune," or "I'd buy stocks from start-up companies, knowing that in the future I'll be worth millions!"

Of course, if you said that if you went back in time, then you would be unable to pay for the gold or stocks because today's money would be worthless, you would have to use money that had dates that agreed with the time period. By bringing reality into the mix, you just became a major buzz kill.

DON'T FORGET THE CHILDREN

AC (a pseudonym) heard about my time slip inquiries and contacted me to share his experience as a young student. He called me mid-afternoon on a Monday. I told him about my project and the phenomenon I was researching. We spoke for about a half-hour; it didn't take long before he felt at ease and decided to meet in person. We agreed to meet locally, at the Arlington Diner.

I didn't know what to expect from AC. Sometimes, you speak to someone who sounds fantastic over the phone, but when you meet them in person, they look like an escapee from a mental asylum, which makes you question everything they say. AC arrived on time and was well-dressed with a conservative haircut. So far, so good.

I knew I was about to get a good story from him. We started with small talk and then ordered our lunch. We both had the cheeseburger deluxe platters. For those not from New Jersey and familiar with diner lingo, that's the cheeseburger and French fries with a few leaves of lettuce and a slice of tomato.

The interview with AC was straightforward because, to this day, he remembered the school trip he and his class took to Washington, DC, in fine detail. He named all his friends and the pretty girls on the trip and even where they sat on the bus! When AC was about to reveal his time slip story to me, his face took on a worried expression. Could he be afraid that I wouldn't believe him? For all he knew, I could be writing stories of mentally challenged people who were delusional and believed in time slips.

I told him that time slip stories are a trendy subject now, talked about frequently on television, in films, and in books. I assured AC that I was sincere and intended to take a fresh approach concerning time slips, one that the reader could relate to their own experience without fear of judgment by others.

AC began by telling me that, at the time of his experience, he was a fourteen-year-old student at St. Cecilia's School in Iselin, New Jersey. His time slip occurred during his 8th-grade class trip to Washington, DC.

AC had a remarkable memory. He not only knew every kid on the bus but also where everyone was seated. To an eighth grader, a trip like this is the best.

They can hang out with their friends, eat junk food, horse around, and check out the girls from the class. They can also take pictures of the buildings or statues to show mom and dad.

The bus dropped off the students in front of the Capitol. What happened next left a mark on AC's soul to this very day. While he was walking up the Capitol stairs with the rest of the class, he looked down and noticed the steps were not worn; they looked new. Yet, he remembered that when he first arrived and began to ascend, they looked worn. He then noticed that the people around him were speaking loudly. AC lifted his head. The light seemed to darken slightly, and he noticed that everyone wore clothing from the late 1800s.

AC froze in his tracks and watched events unfold before his eyes. He certainly didn't count on this when he signed up for the trip. In a few minutes, everything went back to normal. I asked what did he do next?

"I didn't say a word to anybody," he said. Not a word to his school chums, his parents, the St. Cecilia's sisters, or priests who accompanied them on the trip. "NOBODY!"

"I didn't want anyone to think I was crazy," he said.

I never got the impression that he was fabricating any part of his story. Instead, I felt that telling me what happened to him on that day lifted a heavy weight off his shoulders. I'm sure he was relieved that after all these years, someone reached out to him and validated what happened on that trip to Washington, DC. So, it wasn't a bad dream; it was a real thing, and this time slip not only happened to him but also to others.

How many young people have similar experiences but are afraid to share them with family and friends? When an adult carries on about their time slip, they get a pass because they're adults, but let a young boy or girl say that this has happened to them, and then look out! The parental forces encircle them, demanding they come clean, saying it was all made up, and if they insist it happened, threaten them with punishment or take them to a counselor or psychologist to figure out their problem.

AC was wise not to discuss the incident back then, deciding to lock it away in the dark recesses of his mind until years later when he met me at the diner.

The Arlington Diner. Photo by Karl Petry.

What's Next?

Let's face it, trying to explain a time slip to someone is very hard, and in most cases, it's outright impossible. Unless it happens to them, people find it hard to believe such a weird paranormal experience could occur. I understand. If I heard someone like me tell my story of traveling back in time and being where I was, I'd listen but find it hard to believe.

We live in a time when we can get instant answers or explanations for anything we may imagine. If time slips are real, we say, "Show me a video and confirmation from paranormal experts on the internet!"

Earlier, I spoke of rogue waves that came out of nowhere to sink or damage many ships. For centuries, people believed that it was poor seamanship or an excuse to cover the theft of goods on board. No one believed that these waves existed, nor did they believe the stories told of them by sailors. All that changed when a giant wave was recorded on an oil drilling platform off the Norwegian coast on January 1, 1995. After that video was released, all hell broke loose, and the term "rogue wave" was born. We now have "rogue wave" experts.

I believe the same will happen when the existence of time slips is proven to the public's satisfaction. With research and a bit of luck, we'll one day have answers to why it happens, and why it takes place at specific locations and times. This is not just a paranormal phenomenon, but a potential frontier for scientific discovery.

I'm sure the answer is already out there. I'm convinced that someone has the correct theory and is trying to find a way to recreate the conditions to produce a time slip on demand. Getting others to join in with the research will be hard because the discovery of this phenomenon does not yield monetary benefits.

Why spend money on a project like this when there is no conceivable way to profit from it? If you want to prove the existence of time slips and need money to research, you will have to resort to crowd-sourcing sites or grants from colleges or universities. That is, unless you can find a way to make money by dashing back into time for a few minutes.

Sounds unimaginable? On June 7, 2019, NASA offered, for a price, the opportunity for individuals to go to the International Space Station. For a fee of $35,000 per day and a 50-million-dollar charge for the ride there and back, the dream of space travel for private citizens could become a reality. NASA found an excellent way to add cash to the space program and at no risk to themselves. Passengers assumed all liability, and NASA was not responsible for anything that might go wrong.

At times, I may sound like a pessimist. With my lecturing experience over the years, I could see how someone might get that impression. In my defense, when a person signs up to hear a presenter on topics such as ghosts, UFOs, or time slips, it's understood the presenter will be taking you on a journey into an area of special interest that is not a popular subject for the public.

Sadly, on occasion, you'll find a few in the audience who will be loud and opinionated, calling anyone who disagrees with their beliefs "fools," no matter how out in left field their own opinions are. These few can turn a presentation from a happy, positive learning experience into a negative event that brings everyone down. In the end, it will seem as if the event has gone sour, and the presentation that started off fun and optimistic will now have an air of pessimistic gloom.

Things Are Getting Better

As I previously stated, after someone experiences a time slip, they get scared, and when the slip ends, they withdraw within themselves and try never to reveal the incident to anyone. This has been the case for years.

I'm happy to say that things are changing. Recently, more and more people who have experienced time slips have taken to posting their episodes on social media. They no longer retreat within themselves or become incommunicado to family and friends. Rather, they share what happened to them with the world.

I'm very pleased with this development. Investigative television shows have felt the pressure and are taking the time slip phenomenon seriously. This pressure isn't just limited to time slips; it extends to UFOs, Ghosts, and Bigfoot.

Feeling the pressure, countries have taken steps to release years of classified documents previously withheld from the public that are now being shared with the world. Mexico, for example, has been releasing information from its UFO archives and having meetings open to the media and the public. In 2020, the UK's Ministry of Defence formally released secret UFO reports that date back from the 1950s to 2009. Can we expect the same for time slips? I believe we can.

Maybe we should broaden our look at time slips. Rather than focusing on them as random episodes of time that we stumble into, could they be portals that, if studied long enough, lead us to actual time travel? Could discovering the existence of time slips be why the United States government experimented with time travel at Fort Hero on Long Island? Lastly, does Liverpool's Bold Street hold the answer to a possible floating vortex or portal that by chance was an experiment that went bad, like the Philadelphia Experiment of World War II?

If we believe what has been said, experimenting with the invisibility of a warship through high-power oscillating magnetic poles had a disastrous conclusion. Any or all the records of that experiment are still hidden or have been destroyed. Its existence has been denied by the government, and all accounts brought to light of that test were pieced together from oral reports by military and scientific insiders who had first-hand knowledge of the test.

It's like an inverted pyramid; the whole structure is held up by a single point, and what witnesses are saying is true. People who are the respectable pillars of society are singing the same tune. Their account of time slips is in lockstep with all the others. There is a notable lack of extremists or radicals on this issue, only plain folk who will share a very strange happening in their lives.

It seems we've gone full circle from individuals experiencing a time slip to possibly entering a doorway into time itself, even if only for a few minutes. It's like the Wright brothers mastering the first mechanical flight of an airplane in 1903. Their aim was recreation and transportation, but once their flying machine was found to be a dependable, workable device, more uses were imagined, and it was no surprise that the military knocked on their door. The genie was out of the bottle; it was time to supply the wants and needs of a growing nation.

If we discovered the routine of when and where a time slip occurs, the next step would be to wait to see if we could interact with it and hitch a ride to the past, and dare I say, possibly change something in history's past we didn't like? This is the taboo of every science fiction theory of time travel. It's said that to change even the slightest thing in the past can alter the future and disrupt our present. Is this true? I don't know; no one to my knowledge has ever successfully traveled back in time. However, if they did and changed the past, how would we know they did?

The bottom line is that a time slip is NOT the act of traveling in time. It's an interaction of sharing a bit of a time from the past with our own time. We are now at the stage of just trying to bring time slips to the attention of a disbelieving world. Progress in belief and acceptance of this phenomenon is being made, but for now, they're baby steps. We still have a long way to go.

I and the people I interviewed went through a series of uncontrollable human factors. I call it this because it operates just like our midbrain. The midbrain controls our body's functions like motor movement, including auditory and visual processing. These happen automatically and don't need our input to make them function.

Once you find yourself in a time slip, there is a knee-jerk reaction you can't overcome the moment it happens. There are four uncontrollable happenings when your slip happens. (1) Curiosity: The shock of the changes that just appeared before you. (2) Recognition: Trying to figure out where in time you are. (3) Environment: The change in the difference in smells, temperature, and light. And leaving the worst for last, (4) Fear: The possible interaction with the people you encounter with the added heightened anxiety of the possibility you won't return to your own time.

GHOSTS OR TIME SLIPS?

I am familiar with groups that explore old houses, farms, and factories, looking for ghosts. They're often equipped with electronic gear, trying to capture images, shadows, or sounds to validate their ghostly discoveries. It usually starts off with someone reporting a ghost, and then before you know it, an entire crew of enthusiasts stake out the place and wait for something to happen. Sometimes, their stakeout pays off, and they get a blotchy image that may be stationary or moving, and on occasion, they record sounds. However, overall, it's a long wait to get something, and many times, nothing happens at all.

We automatically assume what people see or claim to see are ghosts. We believe that spirits of people may remain on earth after death, hanging around in various buildings or grounds for reasons we are unaware of. Grieving families will sometimes want to contact a loved one who passed, looking for answers or direction for the ones left behind. These people become susceptible to unscrupulous characters, masquerading as mediums and psychics, to capitalize on their grief. Many people fall victim to this horrible fraud and are often cheated out of considerable sums of money. This is a way of life for unsavory characters and has been for many years. I don't see any solution to this problem in the foreseeable future. Educating the public about this is the only way to curb or stop the victimization of people in grief.

Personally, I believe in the existence of ghosts, or spirits, as I prefer to call them. I am not a member of any ghost group and don't stake out buildings or grounds looking for something to happen. When I do take part in an investigation, it's at the personal request of someone troubled by paranormal happenings.

One example was an office in New York City being redecorated. The job was moving at a snail's pace because the workers doing the redecorating kept walking off the job. They had an uneasy feeling working there. They said it felt like ghosts were lurking around them. The tenant whose office was being redecorated wanted to know what was really going on and if the workers' claims had any legitimacy. Also, he was concerned that when he opened for business, would customers, like the workers, have that same feeling of dread? That's when a real in-depth paranormal investigation is called for.

When a situation of this magnitude occurs, I will investigate the case, but seldom alone. The English psychic Paula Roberts from New York City accompanies me. Her talent for this type of work is outstanding. We implement a special, foolproof investigation technique. The people who call us are impressed with this method, and because of our reputation, they know we will never take advantage of their situation. Our investigation is kept strictly between us and the client.

Could some people seeing a time slip mistake it for a ghost? One woman recalling when her ghost group was staking out a closed sanitarium said, "I saw a woman standing in the hall of the hospital wearing dated clothes from '20s. She looked at me surprised that I was there. She stood motionless for about twenty seconds, then turned and walked away, disappearing into a room adjacent to the hall." Another claimed to see his deceased mother slowly walking down his driveway, smiling at him, but she vanished about a minute later. Ghosts? Could be. Time slip vision? Could be. When you think about it, both could be interchangeable. Could we have been mistaken in believing all these images were ghosts since we didn't have knowledge of time slips? It may be time for us to take a fresh look at what we see. If I didn't know about time slips, I would be thinking of ghosts too.

Whenever the subject of ghosts is discussed, we should consider the possibility that the ghostly image seen could have been a time slip.

LET'S GO TO THE SECURITY
CAMERAS

A popular television show reveals the strange and amazing things captured on security cameras, from strange creatures walking around a house to people appearing in a yard and vanishing. We scratch our heads, trying to figure out what the camera caught, to make sense of the footage and come up with a rational explanation of what it could possibly be. After we see it, the next step is to invite family and friends to view the footage to get their opinion.

If the video is good, you can contact the television show and present what you have, to see if they'd be interested in showing it on their program. With luck, the video will be aired. I've watched many of these shows,

111

and blurry, fading images will point in the direction of ghosts. Little skinny people with strange clothing walking around the house lend themselves to being extraterrestrials, and those rascals always seem to pop up when we search for explanations. If it's a hairy animal as tall as a large man, it could very well be Bigfoot.

They usually have an expert on the show who critiques the video and will give a series of opinions of what it could be. Don't expect the expert to be one hundred percent certain what it is. They never will; to do so would be foolish and could hurt their reputation in the long run. If later it becomes apparent that what was shown was staged or the work of pranksters, you and the show will suffer from a lack of credibility, and no one will take you or the show seriously anymore.

What we do know is that on occasion, some phenomena appear and disappear, and we're at a loss as to why this happens.

Maybe what we're seeing is a perfect example of a time slip, a few seconds of an image captured from the past, coming through to our present time. If the camera hadn't recorded it, we would have never known of its existence. If a tree falls in a forest and no one is around to hear it, does it make a sound?

It's my belief that we occasionally and momentarily enter a time from the past. Nothing radical, just a flash of time, that will neither add nor detract from our lives. Mankind could be subject to this phenomenon constantly, but the duration of each episode is so short, that we have no knowledge of it actually happening.

URBAN LEGENDS

No matter what state you live in, you'll hear spooky stories like that of a ghost who walks on a lonely country road; the description of this specter ranges from a woman dressed in a wedding dress, an elderly man, a young boy, or girl, walking alongside the roadway looking for a ride.

As the story unfolds, a driver who is passing by observes this person, stops, and offers this person a ride. When they reach their destination, supposedly a home where the hitchhiker lives, the person in the car vanishes. When the driver goes to the house and tells the people about the rider who vanished, the people from the house are aware of what happened to the rider and tell the driver the sad story of that person who once lived in their house, who died tragically many years ago. At the end of the story, they say, "It looks like they try to make their way home even after death." This makes for a fantastic ghost story, and no matter the variation of the story, it manages to hold the listener's interest.

This story could be based on a real incident, but over time and telling the story again and again, it's embellished to such a degree that it is now a far cry from the original. If we believe the tale could have been based on a real paranormal event, could we also believe the driver picked up a person in a time slip, rather than a ghost?

Proceeding with the premise that the person picked up by the driver was in a time slip, we established that a verbal interaction was made between the two parties. This is very important. As a rule, ghosts are seen and not heard and certainly don't carry on conversations. We know the conversation happened because the driver got their home address from the passenger.

In the many interviews and accounts from those who experienced a time slip episode, they reported interacting with the people from the time slip past. Putting it another way, when a person regresses in time during a time slip and sees faces of people from the past and words are exchanged, it is a good bet the verbal exchange is happening.

If you hear someone telling this ghost story, remember you could be hearing an actual time slip story. You can share your thoughts on time slips, or if you prefer, sit back and enjoy the creepy ghost story.

Right now, time slips are at the top of my list of unusual paranormal happenings. Bringing this phenomenon to the attention of the masses at times seems like a monumental task. It's easy for those who experienced a time slip to want to understand its concept and to be eager to share what happened to them with others.

However, if a person has never experienced it, the concept of time slips, and the person talking about it, are called into question. No matter how much you try, a small part of your audience will be incapable of understanding the concept of time slips. This doesn't make your situation special because anyone who breaks ground on new concepts or theories will go through the same period of questionability from their peers and critics. So, you are in good company.

Once a person makes up their mind, it's almost impossible to change it. No matter what logic or evidence you present, they will only dig in deeper and hold on to their beliefs.

THE VANUATU PEOPLE

It is human nature that with most people, once they commit themselves to an opinion or belief, they stick with it no matter what contrary facts or proof you bring before them. For example, there is the story of a people who live in Vanuatu, a remote island in the South Pacific. During the Second World War, airplanes flew over Vanuatu for the first time. The islanders had never seen airplanes before. Soon, construction crews made their way to the Island, clearing it for a runway. Vanuatu was chosen because it was the perfect location to re-supply the Australian army and to bring goods to the natives of the Island.

Once the landing strip was made, airplanes began to bring in food and supplies to the Island people. To them, magic gave them all this good stuff. They were convinced these big flying things came from a Messiah. Explanations by the government, pilots, and ground crews of what an airplane was and where all the food and cargo were coming from were something they could not understand nor wanted to understand.

When the war was over in 1946, the Australian government patrols discovered what had happened to the people of Vanuatu. The islanders had turned the delivery of supplies by the cargo planes into an actual religion or cult.

Whenever they saw an airplane fly over the Island, they would bring out a large model of an airplane, lay it out on the ground, or hang it on a tree, trying to coax the plane to land. They wouldn't stop there; they would also light fires alongside the runway so the planes could land, just like they did years ago during the war.

Airplanes, to this day, do not land on the Island of Vanuatu. These islanders are stubborn, holding fast to their beliefs. No matter what you tell them, they will not change their minds.

This is the point I'm making about some people: no matter what you show or tell them, they will not budge from their beliefs. If you find yourself in a one-on-one discussion or argument about the topic of time slips, remember this story of the Vanuatu islanders. They are known as the followers of the Cargo Religion.

WORDS FROM A CATHOLIC SISTER

When I attended the third grade at Saint Casimir's School in Newark, NJ, a Catholic Parochial School, the nuns teaching us were Felician Sisters. The Felician order originated from Poland in 1855, came to North America in 1874, and was affiliated with the Roman Catholic Church. On this one day, one of the female students from the class asked our sister, "What happens when you die?" I'll never forget what she said. I expected her to recite chapter and verse the Catholic mantra of going to heaven and spending eternity worshipping Jesus. But she didn't. To my shock, she said that when you die, you start your life all over again. You get a chance to correct all the mistakes you made in this life. If you don't correct all those mistakes,

119

you'll have the opportunity to start over again and keep returning until you correct everything.

After hearing this, I put the question of life after death behind me. Maybe because it sounded good, I wanted to avoid jinxing it by questioning or challenging the notion. If the sister said it, how could it be wrong? Even at such a young age, however, it did make me think of the concept of life or time repeating itself—that life and time weren't final, and the possibility of reliving it was possible.

What the sister said was against all the teachings of the religion she represented. Sadly, I don't remember the sister's name or the student who posed the question to her. This sister took a chance to share her view of eternity with a mere third-grade student. If any of the students had repeated her words to one of the other sisters or a priest, she would have paid dearly for her "life after death" opinion. To the best of my knowledge, that didn't happen. I must give her credit for giving me something to think about for all these years.

It would fit if I applied the time slip factor to what she said. The past repeats itself over and over. Those who experience a time slip will confirm that it is nothing more than time repeating itself.

During a time slip, we're dropped into a scene from the past. Without notice or invitation, we appear. Why? Who are we in this phantom world? If I appear in a year before my birth, it certainly won't be from my past, but then whose?

Time slips are a mystery. To solve this mystery, we should look for clues from all sources and not rule out anything, even if it happens to be a sister from a parochial elementary school from years ago.

Here is food for thought: according to the theory of relativity, the past, present, and future are happening at the same time. In short, time does not flow in an absolute way but depends on the inertial frame of reference of the observer. Past, present, and future coexist in space-time and are interconnected; there is no clear distinction between them. Could this be applied to the sister's story? Could we slide from one time to another without warning or notice? This would be the basis for a time slip.

I'm confident that in the foreseeable future, the answers we are looking for will become known to us. For now, try to keep an open mind and don't let the naysayers get the best of you. It's a long road; buckle yourself in and enjoy the ride.

TIME SLIP REVISITED

We hear about the many time slips on Bold Street in Liverpool. Whenever a radio or television show, blog, or other written account reports on this phenomenon, Bold Street, the site of many time slip incidents, is the usual starting point.

To people outside of the UK, stories of time slips from Liverpool are interesting. Unfortunately, it's a faraway place that only those who live in the UK or visit Liverpool can relate to. When presenting and discussing time slips, I tell of my experience in a Bloomfield, New Jersey, cemetery. It's local, and my audience can easily relate to it and visit the location.

When I finish the story, I'm asked if I ever returned to the site of my time slip. The answer, until recently, has always been no, and the reason is that time slips are terrifying; each minute that I was there seemed like hours. When I returned to the present, I quickly exited the cemetery. Getting away was the only thing on my mind, and fear was a great incentive to keep me or anyone from returning to the scene of the slip.

Just the thought of returning to the cemetery felt dangerous to me. I couldn't help but think about what went through my head. What if the time slip happened again, and I didn't return? I could remain in that past time forever. This is the stuff nightmares are made of. If I were to return to the cemetery, would I relive the slip?

This raises the question; does a time slip happen at the same place more than once? Is there some kind of a vortex that manifests itself by opening and closing at varied timed intervals? Could time slips happen constantly at the same place unnoticed because the slip happens in extremely short durations? If a microsecond slip happened while someone passed by, would they notice it? If the time slip were to extend itself from microseconds to actual seconds or minutes, would that get people's attention? If we accept this explanation of time slip duration, it may be time to revisit all known time slip locations.

Should we start by studying the multiple slip sites on Bold Street? The street is very busy with shops and eateries, so if we proceeded to probe the various locations, we would have a large group of investigators running tests. The investigators and curious bystanders would impact the flow of pedestrian traffic or even block the sidewalks and street. As a result, the efforts to find answers to the time slip question would not be welcomed by the merchants, their customers, or commuters. Not all people believe, understand, or care about time slips. So, to find the cause and effect of time slips, we should bypass any research on the always-busy Bold Street, at least for now.

As mentioned, my time slip occurred at a local cemetery, only a few miles from my home. Except for an occasional visitor, all the folks there are dead and don't mind our company at all. It would be up to me to summon some bravery and revisit this cemetery.

I decided to return, but I wouldn't enter the cemetery alone. I would bring credible observers to watch me and to witness any phenomena, should they occur.

It was late Saturday when I persuaded myself to return to the cemetery and decided who would accompany me. My wife and psychologist, Sueli S. Petry, PhD, was a no-brainer; her personal and professional input would help me observe and understand the event. I included radio personalities, Gary Mantz and Suzanne Mitchell. I've been on their radio show a number of times; they are knowledgeable on the subject, and most importantly, I feel at ease with them.

The next day, we entered Bloomfield Cemetery around 2 p.m. I re-enacted for the crew what happened the day of my time slip, pointing out where each person

(L to R) Gary Mantz, Suzanne Mitchell, Karl Petry, Sueli S. Petry, Ph.D. Photo by Karl Petry.

I saw was standing and repeating the words I heard from the minister.

I circled the entire area with a compass, looking for magnetic anomalies. I didn't find any. We remained at the site for about 45 minutes, searching for anything that was unusual or different. I felt no dizziness, headache, or visual problems; it was a typical day at the cemetery. Although this visitation didn't result in finding answers for me, it was certainly worth the trip. I now feel more comfortable about returning to my time slip site. I'll make it a point to return occasionally to see if there are any changes or developments over time. If anyone wants to join me in doing tests or to conduct their own investigation, I can now bring them there.

Time Slip Overview

We have covered a lot of territory concerning time slips. The subject sounds like something made up because it's rare, and only a handful of people experience it. We have credible accounts of time slips that date back many years. When those incidents were reported or discussed, no one took these sightings seriously and just wrote them off like someone having a bad dream.

Trying to gather information for this publication wasn't easy for me. When conducting my interviews, I found a pattern of behavior that accompanied every person I spoke to. The overwhelming emotion during their time slip was fear. Before and during the telling of their story, each person showed signs of nervousness, like fidgeting in their chair the whole time we spoke. As they told me their story, they watched me closely, trying to get my reaction to it. The obvious question on their mind was, did I believe them? The fear of ridicule was always present at our meetings, and most insisted that I do not use their real name in this book. This caveat was a result of the reactions they got when they told others about their slip story.

One example of this is when a young man who had a time slip told his girlfriend about it. After hearing her boyfriend's story, she showed no interest in what he said and was convinced he made up the story. She became angry at his insistence that his experience was genuine; she was confident that he was fabricating his story to make himself look important. His time slip episode ended their relationship.

This does not mean that if you have a time slip, you should not talk about it. It's essential that you do, but make sure those listening understand what you're talking about. Every day, more people become aware of this phenomenon and post their stories on social media. This will help you find and contact the right people. That's how I was able to reach out to find and interview people who had a time slip experience.

Let's not forget the philosophical component of time slips. To "slip" from one time to another is logically wrong. This brief transport of time breaks all the rules of physics and logic. With time slips, we're dealing with outlandish ideas and theories that seem more like science fiction than reality.

It all comes down to the question: Do time slips exist? The answer is yes. Too many credible witnesses have experienced this, and their descriptions of each of their time slip events were identical.

This is not new; the same controversy popped up when there was talk of remote viewing. Do some people have the ability to view remote places with just their minds? The answer to this is also yes, and we have absolute proof of that. When the opportunity came up to cash in on remote viewing, the film *The Men Who Stare at Goats* was released as a black comedy in 2009. Will it take a film about time slips to bring this subject to the public? I hope not, but it wouldn't surprise me.

When asked, I will continue to speak to the various groups at their gatherings on paranormal subjects. Spooky subjects are very popular, especially ghosts during the Halloween month of October. Everyone loves ghost stories, maybe because they've been exposed to them from childhood. From a cartoon character named Casper to the studio films from the 1930s through today, you can't miss with ghosts.

For the past few years, I've tried to shy away from talking about ghosts and instead introduce audiences to the new topic of time slips. The reaction has been favorable. Time slips are a new subject that few have heard of. When I tell of the many time slip examples, they listen intently, hanging on every word, and no one in the audience is bored. At the end of the presentation, question after question will be asked until we run out of time, forcing the end of the program.

You would think only those who have never experienced a time slip would have questions about it, but surprisingly, it's the opposite. Those who experienced a time slip event want to know what it is. Why did it happen to them? Will it happen to them again? Finally, is it dangerous? We're now bobbing and weaving through a labyrinth of cynics and experts in various scientific fields trying to get those answers. Let's face it: we're still in the discovery stage, seeking whatever information we can get on this subject.

Final Word

Those who experience a time slip are special people. They've traveled to a singular place, a trip through time for a few moments. It is a road less traveled, and only a few have weathered it.

To all those with whom I had the pleasure of interviewing, I thank you. Your stories confirmed what I saw and felt during my own time slip.

I hope the time we spent during our interviews has helped you better understand this book's purpose. Being upfront and candid about your experience made my job much easier.

I refrained from retelling each of your stories because doing so would only be repetitive and frustrate readers who have never experienced a time slip. The word is getting out there, and with the additional publicity, it could lay the groundwork for a successful future study of this phenomenon.

Hearing time slip stories from the United Kingdom that were identical to those of the United States wasn't really surprising. It proved to me that this phenomenon was the same everywhere.

The United Kingdom is ancient compared to the United States, which may be a factor in the ubiquity of time slips. While traveling with our UK hosts, Dean and Stuart, we were given a dose of reality about the ages of the roads and buildings there.

My home in the US will celebrate its 100th year this coming May. When I tell my friends and family about this, they're surprised at its age. Only a few homes make it to one hundred years. Yet, average homes in many areas of the UK could easily be over two hundred years old! I've considered this extended age of their society when I'm piecing together possible reasons for the manifestation of the time slips.

Lastly, to those I've met from the United Kingdom, a special thanks for the kindness you've shown to this writer from across the pond. Our accents may have been different, but we certainly understood each other.

Karl Petry

About the Author

Karl Petry is known for his accurate clairvoyance, his ability to tune into the past via retrocognition, and the ability to read objects and photographs via psychometry. He participates in paranormal investigations and has worked with other investigators to assess haunted locations and to analyze photographic evidence of paranormal phenomena.

Karl sharpened his abilities with Ingo Swann, the New York City psychic who created the foundation for the U.S. government's classified program in remote viewing.

Karl is an independent film producer operating in the New York metropolitan area. Karl's work on one paranormal investigation was so compelling that he produced a film docudrama based on it to try to capture and share his personal experience.[1]

Karl has been a guest speaker at the New Jersey City State University; various New Jersey high schools; the Stroudsburg Public Library (Stroudsburg, PA); the

---

1 *The Ghosts of Angela Webb*

New Jersey Freemason Lodges in Nutley, Rutherford, Morristown, Lyndhurst and Ramsey, NJ; the New Jersey Paranormal Association Meetings, held at the Hamilton Library in Hamilton, NJ, and its yearly conference. He has been a frequent lecturer at the annual Pennsylvania Paranormal Society in Mt. Joy, PA.

Karl was honored to present at the North Arlington Woman's Club and the New Jersey State Federation of Women's Clubs of GFWC. He gave the keynote address at the Eastern Monroe Public Library's Book Expo in Stroudsburg, PA.

Karl has made numerous appearances on radio, television and web shows such as *In the Psychic Flow* with Carolan Carey (Sarasota, Florida), and the *Mantz and Mitchell* AM radio show, Seattle, Washington.

Made in the USA
Middletown, DE
18 November 2024

64698147R00090